Racial Profiling

Racial Profiling

David L. Hudson Jr.

SERIES EDITOR
Alan Marzilli, M.A., J.D.

CHELSEA HOUSE
PUBLISHERS
An imprint of Infobase Publishing

Racial Profiling

Chelsea House
An imprint of Infobase Publishing
132 West 31st Street
New York, NY 10001

Library of Congress Cataloging-in-Publication Data
Hudson, David L., 1969–
 Racial profiling / by David L. Hudson.
 p. cm.
 Includes bibliographical references and index.
 ISBN 978-1-60413-717-0
 1. Racial profiling in law enforcement—United States. 2. Race discrimination—Law and legislation—United States. I. Title.
 HV8141.H83 2010
 363.2'308900973—dc22
                    2010006598

Chelsea House books are available at special discounts when purchased in bulk quantities for businesses, associations, institutions, or sales promotions. Please call our Special Sales Department in New York at (212) 967-8800 or (800) 322-8755.

You can find Chelsea House on the World Wide Web at http://www.chelseahouse.com.

Text design by Keith Trego
Cover design by Alicia Post
Composition by EJB Publishing Services
Cover printed by Bang Printing, Brainerd, MN
Book printed and bound by Bang Printing, Brainerd, MN
Date printed: December 2010
Printed in the United States of America

10 9 8 7 6 5 4 3 2 1

FOREWORD

Alan Marzilli, M.A., J.D.
Birmingham, Alabama

The POINT/COUNTERPOINT series offers the reader a greater understanding of some of the most controversial issues in contemporary American society—issues such as capital punishment, immigration, gay rights, and gun control. We have looked for the most contemporary issues and have included topics—such as the controversies surrounding "blogging"—that we could not have imagined when the series began.

In each volume, the author has selected an issue of particular importance and set out some of the key arguments on both sides of the issue. Why study both sides of the debate? Maybe you have yet to make up your mind on an issue, and the arguments presented in the book will help you to form an opinion. More likely, however, you will already have an opinion on many of the issues covered by the series. There is always the chance that you will change your opinion after reading the arguments for the other side. But even if you are firmly committed to an issue—for example, school prayer or animal rights—reading both sides of the argument will help you to become a more effective advocate for your cause. By gaining an understanding of opposing arguments, you can develop answers to those arguments.

Perhaps more importantly, listening to the other side sometimes helps you see your opponent's arguments in a more human way. For example, Sister Helen Prejean, one of the nation's most visible opponents of capital punishment, has been deeply affected by her interactions with the families of murder victims. By seeing the families' grief and pain, she understands much better why people support the death penalty, and she is able to carry out her advocacy with a greater sensitivity to the needs and beliefs of death penalty supporters.

The books in the series include numerous features that help the reader to gain a greater understanding of the issues. Real-life examples illustrate the human side of the issues. Each chapter also includes excerpts from relevant laws, court cases, and other material, which provide a better foundation for understanding the arguments. The

volumes contain citations to relevant sources of law and information, and an appendix guides the reader through the basics of legal research, both on the Internet and in the library. Today, through free Web sites, it is easy to access legal documents, and these books might give you ideas for your own research.

Studying the issues covered by the POINT/COUNTERPOINT series is more than an academic activity. The issues described in the books affect all of us as citizens. They are the issues that today's leaders debate and tomorrow's leaders will decide. While all of the issues covered in the POINT/COUNTERPOINT series are controversial today, and will remain so for the foreseeable future, it is entirely possible that the reader might one day play a central role in resolving the debate. Today it might seem that some debates—such as capital punishment and abortion—will never be resolved.

However, our nation's history is full of debates that seemed as though they never would be resolved, and many of the issues are now well settled—at least on the surface. In the nineteenth century, abolitionists met with widespread resistance to their efforts to end slavery. Ultimately, the controversy threatened the union, leading to the Civil War between the northern and southern states. Today, while a public debate over the merits of slavery would be unthinkable, racism persists in many aspects of society.

Similarly, today nobody questions women's right to vote. Yet at the beginning of the twentieth century, suffragists fought public battles for women's voting rights, and it was not until the passage of the Nineteenth Amendment in 1920 that the legal right of women to vote was established nationwide.

What makes an issue controversial? Often, controversies arise when most people agree that there is a problem but disagree about the best way to solve it. There is little argument that poverty is a major problem in the United States, especially in inner cities and rural areas. Yet, people disagree vehemently about the best way to address the problem. To some, the answer is social programs, such as welfare, food stamps, and public housing. However, many argue that such subsidies encourage dependence on government benefits while unfairly penalizing those who work and pay taxes, and that the real solution is to require people to support themselves.

American society is in a constant state of change, and sometimes modern practices clash with what many consider to be "traditional values," which are often rooted in conservative political views or religious beliefs. Many blame high crime rates, and problems such as poverty, illiteracy, and drug use on the breakdown of the traditional family structure of a married mother and father raising their children. Since the "sexual revolution" of the 1960s and 1970s, sparked in part by the widespread availability of the birth control pill, marriage rates have declined, and the number of children born outside of marriage has increased. The sexual revolution led to controversies over birth control, sex education, and other issues, most prominently abortion. Similarly, the gay rights movement has been challenged as a threat to traditional values. While many gay men and lesbians want to have the same right to marry and raise families as heterosexuals, many politicians and others have challenged gay marriage and adoption as a threat to American society.

Sometimes, new technology raises issues that we have never faced before, and society disagrees about the best solution. Are people free to swap music online, or does this violate the copyright laws that protect songwriters and musicians' ownership of the music that they create? Should scientists use "genetic engineering" to create new crops that are resistant to disease and pests and produce more food, or is it too risky to use a laboratory to create plants that nature never intended? Modern medicine has continued to increase the average lifespan—which is now 77 years, up from under 50 years at the beginning of the twentieth century—but many people are now choosing to die in comfort rather than living with painful ailments in their later years. For doctors, this presents an ethical dilemma: should they allow their patients to die? Should they assist patients in ending their own lives painlessly?

Perhaps the most controversial issues are those that implicate a Constitutional right. The Bill of Rights—the first 10 Amendments to the U.S. Constitution—spells out some of the most fundamental rights that distinguish our democracy from other nations with fewer freedoms. However, the sparsely worded document is open to interpretation, with each side saying that the Constitution is on their side. The Bill of Rights was meant to protect individual liberties; however, the needs of some individuals clash with society's needs. Thus, the Constitution often serves as a battleground between individuals and government officials seeking to protect society in some way. The First Amendment's guarantee of "freedom of speech" leads to some very difficult questions. Some forms of expression—such as burning an American flag—lead to public outrage, but are protected by the First Amendment. Other types of expression that most people find objectionable—such as child pornography—are not protected by the Constitution. The question is not only where to draw the line, but whether drawing lines around constitutional rights threatens our liberty.

The Bill of Rights raises many other questions about individual rights and societal "good." Is a prayer before a high school football game an "establishment of religion" prohibited by the First Amendment? Does the Second Amendment's promise of "the right to bear arms" include concealed handguns? Does stopping and frisking someone standing on a known drug corner constitute "unreasonable search and seizure" in violation of the Fourth Amendment? Although the U.S. Supreme Court has the ultimate authority in interpreting the U.S. Constitution, its answers do not always satisfy the public. When a group of nine people—sometimes by a five-to-four vote—makes a decision that affects hundreds of millions of others, public outcry can be expected. For example, the Supreme Court's 1973 ruling in *Roe v. Wade* that abortion is protected by the Constitution did little to quell the debate over abortion.

Whatever the root of the controversy, the books in the POINT/COUNTERPOINT series seek to explain to the reader the origins of the debate, the current state of the law, and the arguments on either side of the debate. Our hope in creating this series is that readers will be better informed about the issues facing not only our politicians, but all of our nation's citizens, and become more actively involved in resolving these debates, as voters, concerned citizens, journalists, or maybe even elected officials.

This volume examines a longstanding controversy that has taken on additional dimensions in recent years. For decades, civil rights groups have alleged that police disproportionately target members of minority groups, and it is often said that "driving while black or brown" puts one at risk of harassment. This volume looks at such issues from the viewpoints of both civil libertarians and law enforcement agencies—the latter of whom argue that what is perceived as racial bias is really good police work based on intuition and experience.

While discussions of racial profiling have traditionally involved African-American citizens, profiling based on Arab or Hispanic origin has become possibly even more controversial. Since the terrorist attacks of September 11, 2001, the general approach to preventing future attacks has been to subject all travelers, visitors to federal buildings, and the like to increased scrutiny. Some critics have charged that such evenhanded tactics inconvenience society at large at the expense of political correctness. Singling out people per-ceived as Arab or Muslim, however, might reinforce stereotypes and would ignore domestic terrorists such as Oklahoma City bomber Timothy McVeigh. In 2010, Arizona sparked a national controversy by passing a law that increased the authority of local law enforce-ment officials to verify individuals' immigration status. Supporters say that the law addresses the enormous problems generated by illegal immigration, while detractors worry that legal immigrants and natural-born citizens will be subjected to harassment.

An Overview of Racial Profiling

In July 2009, Harvard University professor and scholar Henry Louis Gates Jr., who is the head of the university's W.E.B. Du Bois Institute for African and African American Research, returned to his home in Cambridge, Massachusetts. Gates, who had been traveling in China, could not open his front door, as the lock was apparently broken, perhaps from an aborted robbery attempt while he was out of town. Gates and his driver, both African-American men, then tried to force open his front door.

A neighbor called the police, reporting that two men were attempting to break into the door of a nearby home. The local police came to the home in the predominantly white neighborhood, and an officer asked Gates for identification. Gates became agitated at being asked by the police to show identification when he was at his own home.[1] The agitation escalated into a heated dispute between Gates and the police officers.

Accounts differ, but the result was that a white police officer, Sergeant James Crowley, arrested Gates for disorderly conduct. Gates claimed that he was subjected to racial profiling. After a few hours at the jail, he was released. Given Gates's prominence, the incident became national news. The issue escalated after President Barack Obama suggested that the police had "acted stupidly" and that "it doesn't make sense to arrest a guy in his own home if he's not causing a serious disturbance."[2] News reports later revealed that Sergeant Crowley had taught a law enforcement class on racial profiling. President Obama later phoned Crowley and apologized for his remarks. "I want to make clear that in my choice of words I think I unfortunately gave an impression that I was maligning the Cambridge Police Department or Sergeant Crowley specifically—and I could have calibrated those words differently," Obama said. "And I told this to Sergeant Crowley."[3] The president said that Crowley probably overreacted but so did Gates.

The Gates controversy, however, once again thrust into the public spotlight the question of racial profiling, a deeply divisive subject that usually splits people along racial lines. A CNN poll conducted shortly after the incident found that people differed dramatically based on race with respect to the Gates-Crowley incident: 59 percent of blacks thought that Crowley acted stupidly, while only 29 percent of whites thought so.

Not all instances of racial profiling lead to a person being released in only a few hours. Professor Gates is a prominent person who was able to quickly contact his friend Charles Ogletree, a high-powered attorney and law professor. Sometimes racial profiling can lead to arrests that are not even valid or justified. In Tulia, Texas, a corrupt undercover law enforcement official named Tom Coleman targeted poor blacks for violations of drug laws in 1999. Coleman arrested 46 people on drug charges—39 of whom were black. (The whites Coleman

President Barack Obama *(right)* talks with Sergeant James Crowley *(second from right)* and Professor Henry Louis Gates Jr. *(second from left)*, alongside Vice President Joe Biden *(left)* as they share beers on the South Lawn of the White House in Washington, D.C., on July 30, 2009. The men met at the so-called "Beer Summit" in an effort to defuse the controversy surrounding the professor's arrest by Crowley outside Gates's home earlier that month.

arrested were people who associated with blacks in the town.) It was bad enough that Coleman targeted people based on their race. What made this pattern of behavior even more egregious was that many of these defendants were apparently innocent. Despite their innocence, prosecutors obtained convictions or plea bargains for 38 defendants, whose sentences ranged from probation to 341 years in prison.[4] The defendants eventually sued Swisher County, Texas, and received a seven-figure settlement. Tulia became a national scandal and further shone the spotlight on the dangers of racial profiling.[5]

Not a New Phenomenon

Though the term may be new, racial profiling is not a new phenomenon. In 1901, Leon Czolgosz, an anarchist, sought to assassinate President William McKinley. He traveled to Buffalo, New York, after hearing that McKinley was going to appear in public there and give a speech. Security officers neglected to appreciate the threat that Czolgosz might present, because they were focused on a large black man standing right behind Czolgosz named Jim Parker. As it turned out, Parker was a former law enforcement official, while Czolgosz was an assassin. Because President McKinley's security detail focused on the large black man, rather than the smaller white man, Czolgosz managed to fire two shots at McKinley, who later died of his wounds. Coincidentally, it was Parker who managed to tackle Czolgosz, preventing a third shot from hitting McKinley.[6]

During World War II, leading U.S. officials approved of the starkest form of racial profiling when they ordered the internment of Japanese nationals and Japanese-American citizens following the Japanese navy's surprise attack on the U.S. naval base at Pearl Harbor in Hawaii on December 7, 1941. Officials claimed that the extreme measures were necessary because of national security concerns with the war effort. Today, many claim that national security concerns in the wake of the terrorist attacks of September 11, 2001, by radical Islamic fundamentalists require the profiling of men of Middle Eastern or Arab descent who may be terrorists.

Not all racial profiling, however, occurs in the vortex of national security. Many have warned of the phenomenon of "driving while black," "driving while Mexican," or "flying while Arab." The problem became pervasive enough that the U.S. Department of Justice issued a fact sheet on racial profiling.[7] Critics of racial profiling assert that it violates the basic principle of equal protection that is found in the Fourteenth Amendment. The Equal Protection Clause provides that no government officials shall "deny to any person . . . the equal protection of the laws." This means that the government should not treat similarly situated individuals differently based on race, religion, or other differences.

On the other hand, just because a government official has subjected a suspect to some type of search does not mean that the decision was based on an impermissible racial consideration. Police officers, particularly, often must make quick judgments based on their experience. Heather MacDonald writes, for example, that the "Driving While Black belief is pervasive, powerful, and false."[8]

What Is Racial Profiling?

Criminologists and law enforcement agencies often compile profiles of people who commit certain types of crimes. This is called criminal profiling, and it has helped lead to the arrests of countless criminals. There are hijacker profiles, serial killer profiles, sex offender profiles, and many others. Criminal profiling refers to the gathering of information to see if specific crimes occur in specific types of ways and what types of people typically commit these crimes. Criminal profiling is considered to be a legitimate, necessary, and valued part of law enforcement.

THE LETTER OF THE LAW

West Virginia's Legal Definition of Racial Profiling

The term *racial profiling* means the practice of a law-enforcement officer relying, to any degree, on race, ethnicity, or national origin in selecting which individuals to subject to routine investigatory activities, or in deciding upon the scope and substance of law-enforcement activity following the initial routine investigatory activity. *Racial profiling* does not include reliance on race, ethnicity, or national origin in combination with other identifying factors when the law-enforcement officer is seeking to apprehend a specific suspect whose race, ethnicity, or national origin is part of the description of the suspect.

Source: W.Va. Code, Section 30-29-10(b)(3).

The term *racial profiling*, however, has negative connotations and occurs when law enforcement establishes profiles largely on the basis of race. Amnesty International U.S.A. offers the following definition of racial profiling:

> the targeting of individuals and groups by law enforcement officials, even partially, on the basis of race, ethnicity, national origin, or religion, except where there is trustworthy information, relevant to the locality and timeframe, that links persons belonging to one of the aforementioned groups to an identified criminal incident or scheme.[9]

The state of Washington defines racial profiling as "the illegal use of race or ethnicity as a factor in deciding to stop and question, take enforcement action, arrest, or search a person or vehicle with or without a legal basis under the United States Constitution or Washington state Constitution."[10]

The Department of Justice reports that "racial profiling rests on the erroneous assumption that any particular individual of one race or ethnicity is more likely to engage in misconduct than any particular individual of other races or ethnicities."[11] While the report says that broad generalizations or stereotyping of races is prohibited, it also notes that if any investigative or criminal report provides specific racial information, then it is not racial profiling to use that information in landing suspects.

Sometimes it is difficult to separate criminal profiling from racial profiling. One U.S. law enforcement expert explained: "The thing about criminal profiling is you will often find an ethnic group in control for a specific type of crime. For example, Italians on the East Coast were heavily involved in racketeering. In Houston, the Jamaican Posse controlled crack-cocaine distribution."[12]

Sometimes it is hard to draw the line between acceptable criminal profiling and impermissible racial profiling. For example, it has statistically been shown that a sizable number of serial killers have tended to be white men. Does this mean that law enforcement officials may target white men when searching for a serial killer as a legitimate criminal profile, or would this be an example of impermissible racial profiling?

Furthermore, it is often hard to know what actually motivated an officer to stop and frisk or search one person over another. The decision could be based on a variety of factors. If the officer identifies seven different factors, including race, as to why he or she searched a suspect, is that racial profiling? Reasonable minds can differ.

Department of Justice Fact Sheet on Racial Profiling

Stereotyping Certain Races as Having a Greater Propensity to Commit Crimes Is Absolutely Prohibited. Some have argued that overall discrepancies in crime rates among racial groups could justify using race as a factor in general traffic enforcement activities and would produce a greater number of arrests for non-traffic offenses (e.g. narcotics trafficking). We emphatically reject this view. It is patently unacceptable and thus prohibited under this guidance for federal law enforcement officers to engage in racial profiling.

Acting on Specific Suspect Identification Does Not Constitute Impermissible Stereotyping. The situation is different when a federal officer acts on the personal identifying characteristics of potential suspects, including age, sex, ethnicity, or race. Common sense dictates that when a victim or witness describes the assailant as being of a particular race, authorities may properly limit their search for suspects to persons of that race. In such circumstances, the federal officer is not acting on a generalized assumption about persons of different races; rather, the officer is helping locate a specific individual previously identified as involved in crime.

Source: Department of Justice, "Fact Sheet: Racial Profiling," June 17, 2003, p. 3, http://www.justice.gov/opa/pr/2003/June/racial_profiling_fact_sheet.pdf.

Racial Profiling Controversies
Examined in This Book

This book examines racial profiling and provides perspective from both sides of the issue. It looks at three specific areas in which racial profiling accusations have repeatedly surfaced. The first deals with the "war on drugs" and racial profiling. There are widespread accusations that the police have targeted minorities in enforcing the nation's drug laws. This issue began in the 1970s with the creation of the so-called drug courier profile. Supporters contend that the drug courier profile was a legitimate law enforcement technique based on the experience of seasoned agents with the Drug Enforcement Administration (DEA). Opponents counter that the drug courier profile amounted to stark racial profiling and often criminalized innocent behavior. It is important to realize that while the controversy over the drug courier profile began in the 1970s, it is still with us today.

The second issue involves the profiling of men of Middle Eastern or Arab descent in the wake of the horrific terrorist attacks of September 11, 2001. On that day, 19 Middle Eastern men hijacked four commercial airliners and flew them into the World Trade Center in New York City, the Pentagon outside Washington, D.C., and a field in rural Pennsylvania. The heinous attacks took almost 3,000 lives. Some argue that law enforcement and those responsible for national security would be foolish not to focus on suspects hailing from predominantly Arab nations or even Arab-American terrorists. Others counter that terrorists come in all colors, races, and ethnicities and that officials should instead focus solely on behavioral profiling.

The third issue examined in this book deals with the pressing question of illegal immigration and the rapidly growing Latino population. Many illegal immigrants travel into the United States across the U.S.-Mexico border. Some contend that Border Patrol agents must consider race and ethnicity, given the sheer number of illegal immigrants who are Hispanic. Others counter that racial profiling dehumanizes Latinos and subjects them to unnecessary harassment by police officials. This issue is front and center in the news, given the controversy over the Immigration and Customs Enforcement (ICE) agreements that the federal government has signed with numerous local law enforcement agencies. This program empowers local law enforcement officials with the ability to enforce the nation's immigration laws. Supporters of these agreements contend that they are necessary to protect national security and enforce immigration laws. Detractors contend that the ICE agreements lead to more abject racial profiling and assault on immigrants and people of Latino origins.

The Drug Courier Profile Is Effective in Combating the War on Drugs

A man pays cash at the airport for a one-way ticket from Los Angeles to Cincinnati and then another one-way ticket to return to Los Angeles only 12 hours later. He checks no luggage even though he is flying across the country. The man leaves a bogus cell phone number contact with his ticket information. Law enforcement knows that a major drug pipeline begins in Los Angeles with people traveling from there to several cities in the Midwest and the South. Upon exiting the plane in the terminal, the man appears very nervous. He immediately heads to a pay phone to make a call.

An experienced agent with the Drug Enforcement Administration (DEA) spots the man. He also notices that the man is wearing a lot of jewelry and a designer sweat suit. This agent has worked in narcotics for many years. He has also received training at the DEA about a "drug courier profile." The agent does not consider the man's race but rather focuses on all of the above-mentioned factors. He approaches the man with another agent. Eventually, the man consents to a search of his bag, which reveals that he is carrying more than 500 grams of cocaine.

This story has played out in airports, highways, bus terminals, trains, and other places of public transportation for the last several decades. Critics sometimes charge that the tactics of law enforcement amount to impermissible racial profiling, believing that the drug courier profile serves as a convenient mask for rank discrimination against minorities. What the critics fail to mention, however, is that these efforts have resulted in the interdiction and arrest of individuals carrying illegal narcotics that impose untold costs upon millions and millions of U.S. citizens. The critics also fail to mention that the use of the drug courier profile helps law enforcement officials protect the nation and enforce federal, state, and local laws. "Cops are profiling all the time, your good cops; unfortunately, now that's developing a bad name," William J. Bratton, former commissioner of the police departments in Boston, New York City, and Los Angeles, remarked to the *New York Times*. "Whether they call it profiling, or street smarts, awareness—whatever the names might be—profiling is essential."[1]

DEA agents created the drug courier profile to combat a rampant increase in drug trafficking.

In the 1970s, two DEA agents, Paul Markonni and John Marcello, decided to use profiling to fight the war on drugs, particularly in airports in larger cities known to be source cities for drugs. They talked with other DEA agents, defendants in drug possession and distribution cases, and airline workers to determine common characteristics associated with passengers who may be transporting illegal drugs.[2]

Markonni and Marcello noticed that many of the drug traffickers they had encountered and had placed under surveillance exhibited similar characteristics. At the airport, these individuals usually paid for their tickets in cash with rolls of bills, carried their luggage, had an unusual itinerary (meaning they often flew back and forth with little or no overnight stays), and appeared extremely nervous. In 1982, a federal appeals court described this profile as a "valuable administrative tool in guiding law enforcement officers toward individuals on whom the officers should focus their attention in order to determine whether there is a basis for a specific and articulable suspicion that the particular individual is smuggling drugs."[3]

In the first six years of the profile's use at Miami International Airport, the Metro-Dade County Police Department arrested more than 1,000 people and seized more than $1 billion worth of narcotics. Marcello—called "the Godfather" of the drug courier profile program—wrote: "Drug courier profiles work when officers are properly trained, period."[4] The profile is really nothing more than a set of characteristics and pooled knowledge of various law enforcement officials to identify possible violators. To combat the scourge of drugs, officers must be able to monitor and identify suspicious activities.[5] In one federal drug case, Markonni identified seven primary characteristics of the profile and four secondary characteristics. A federal appeals court explained:

> At the suppression hearing Agent Markonni identified seven "primary characteristics" and four "secondary characteristics" that make up the Markonni drug courier profile. . . . The seven primary characteristics are: (1) arrival from or departure to an identified source city; (2) carrying little or no luggage, or large quantities of empty suitcases; (3) unusual itinerary, such as a rapid turnaround time for a very lengthy airplane trip; (4) use of an alias; (5) carrying unusually large amounts of currency in the many thousands of dollars, usually on their person, in briefcases or bags; (6) purchasing

airline tickets with a large amount of small denomination currency; and (7) unusual nervousness beyond that ordinarily exhibited by passengers.

The secondary characteristics are (1) the almost exclusive use of public transportation, particularly taxi-cabs, in departing from the airport; (2) immediately making a telephone call after deplaning; (3) leaving a

FROM THE BENCH

United States v. Mendenhall, 446 U.S. 544, 562-563 (1980)

The public has a compelling interest in detecting those who would traffic in deadly drugs for personal profit. Few problems affecting the health and welfare of our population, particularly our young, cause greater concern than the escalating use of controlled substances. Much of the drug traffic is highly organized and conducted by sophisticated criminal syndicates. The profits are enormous. And many drugs, including heroin, may be easily concealed. As a result, the obstacles to detection of illegal conduct may be unmatched in any other area of law enforcement.

To meet this pressing concern, the Drug Enforcement Administration since 1974 has assigned highly skilled agents to the Detroit Airport as part of a nation-wide program to intercept drug couriers transporting narcotics between major drug sources and distribution centers in the United States. Federal agents have developed "drug courier profiles" that describe the characteristics generally associated with narcotics traffickers. For example, because the Drug Enforcement Administration believes that most drugs enter Detroit from one of four "source" cities (Los Angeles, San Diego, Miami, or New York), agents pay particular attention to passengers who arrive from those places.... During the first 18 months of the program, agents watching the Detroit Airport searched 141 persons in 96 encounters. They found controlled substances in 77 of the encounters and arrested 122 persons.... When two of these agents stopped the respondent in February 1976, they were carrying out a highly specialized law enforcement operation designed to combat the serious societal threat posed by narcotics distribution.

false or fictitious call-back telephone number with the airline being utilized; and (4) excessively frequent travel to source or distribution cities.[6]

The U.S. Supreme Court has approved of the use of the drug courier profile.

Contrary to what critics of the drug courier profile program suggest, these characteristics are not the result of racial discrimination; rather they are the collective knowledge of expert law enforcement officers in the field. In fact, the U.S. Supreme Court has recognized the value of the drug courier profile. In 1980, the Court decided the case of *United States v. Mendenhall*.[7] A young woman named Sylvia Mendenhall arrived at the Detroit Metropolitan Airport on an early flight from Los Angeles. She was the last person to get off the plane, appeared very nervous upon exiting the terminal, and bypassed the baggage area to check in for another flight. Furthermore, officers discovered that she used the alias of "Annette Ford" on her ticket.[8]

Two experienced DEA officers decided to question Mendenhall, particularly after noticing that she quickly bypassed the baggage area to travel via another airline. The officers approached her and asked her a few questions. Mendenhall appeared very nervous and consented to a search, which revealed that she was carrying two packets of heroin. The Court determined that the agents did not violate Mendenhall's Fourth Amendment right to be free from unreasonable searches and seizures.[9] The Court also did not discredit the use of the drug courier profile by the experienced agents.

In his concurring opinion, Justice Lewis Powell praised the law enforcement method of using the drug courier profile:

> The public interest in preventing drug traffic is great, and the intrusion upon the respondent's privacy was minimal. The specially trained agents acted pursuant to a well-planned, and effective, federal law enforcement

program. They observed respondent engaging in conduct that they reasonably associated with criminal activity. Furthermore, the events occurred in an airport known to be frequented by drug couriers.[10]

The Court again approved of the drug courier profile almost a decade later in *United States v. Sokolow*.[11] Andrew Sokolow traveled by plane from Honolulu, Hawaii, to Miami, Florida, a known drug city, and back again, after purchasing tickets worth $2,100 from a roll of $20 bills. He traveled under an alias and

FROM THE BENCH

United States v. Sokolow, 490 U.S. 1, 8-10 (1989)

[T]he factors in this case that the Court of Appeals treated as merely "probabilistic" . . . have probative significance. Paying $2,100 in cash for two airplane tickets is out of the ordinary, and it is even more out of the ordinary to pay that sum from a roll of $20 bills containing nearly twice that amount of cash. Most business travelers, we feel confident, purchase airline tickets by credit card or check so as to have a record for tax or business purposes, and few vacationers carry with them thousands of dollars in $20 bills. We also think the agents had a reasonable ground to believe that respondent was traveling under an alias; the evidence was by no means conclusive, but it was sufficient to warrant consideration. While a trip from Honolulu to Miami, standing alone, is not a cause for any sort of suspicion, here there was more: surely few residents of Honolulu travel from that city for 20 hours to spend 48 hours in Miami during the month of July.

Any one of these factors is not by itself proof of any illegal conduct and is quite consistent with innocent travel. But we think taken together they amount to reasonable suspicion. . . .

We do not agree with respondent that our analysis is somehow changed by the agents' belief that his behavior was consistent with one of the DEA's "drug courier profiles." A court sitting to determine the existence of reasonable suspicion must require the agent to articulate the factors leading to that conclusion, but the fact that these factors may be set forth in a "profile" does not somehow detract from their evidentiary significance as seen by a trained agent.

declined to check any luggage. He also appeared very nervous during the trip, and his return tickets required him to fly back to Hawaii in only 48 hours, despite the long nature of the flight. Federal agents believed he fit a drug courier profile. They were correct, as a later search revealed that Sokolow was carrying more than 1,000 grams of cocaine.[12]

Sokolow contended that officers violated his Fourth Amendment rights because they did not have probable cause or reasonable suspicion to search him and his belongings. A federal district court disagreed and denied his motion to suppress evidence. A federal appeals court, however, reversed the district court's decision, finding that the use of the drug courier profile was problematic. The government then appealed to the U.S. Supreme Court. In an opinion written by Chief Justice William Rehnquist, the Court determined that the agents did have reasonable suspicion to believe that Sokolow was a drug trafficker. The Court noted all of the factors that caused a reviewing federal agent to claim that Sokolow fit the drug courier profile. And there was a reason Sokolow fit the drug courier profile—he was a major drug courier.

The drug courier profile is a necessary weapon in the war on drugs.

The illegal drug problem in the United States has, if anything, worsened over the years. People still smuggle drugs into the country on airplanes, in cars, and through various other methods. Courts and legislators should not hamstring dedicated law enforcement officials from using whatever insights, perceptions, and profiles they have gleaned from their years of hands-on experience.

Some recent court decisions still recognize the need for drug courier profiles as a necessary weapon. One court recently rejected a drug defendant's challenge to the introduction of drug courier profile evidence in his case. The defendant had four cell phones, and the defense counsel asked a police officer whether there was anything illegal about having four cell phones. On redirect examination, the prosecutor asked the officer whether drug dealers often carry multiple cell phones, a known drug courier characteristic. The federal appeals court said there was nothing improper about eliciting that drug courier profile characteristic.[13]

Legal commentator Brian A. Wilson writes that "the development of the drug courier profile has provided the means to effectuate protection of the public, although its ultimate success will require absolute endorsement by the judiciary."[14] Unfortunately, the drug courier profile gets criticized as an impermissible form of racial profiling. The drug courier profile does not single out members of a specific race or ethnic group.

QUOTABLE

Legal Commentator Brian A. Wilson

Since the drug trafficker possesses the extraordinary ability to camouflage himself among ordinary airline passengers, the difficulty inherent in identifying drug traffickers commands, rather than merely justifies, use of the drug courier profile to distinguish the guilty party from the innocent traveler. The legitimate government objective of preventing the flow of illegal drugs within this country outweighs the minimal intrusion upon the public, especially when officers employ drug-sniffing canines to search the luggage of trafficking suspects.

Effective law enforcement requires the preservation of the totality of the circumstances approach and the examination of each case based on its own facts. The automatic dismissal of the relevance of particular profile characteristics violates this standard. Courts must thus abandon the presumption that certain characteristics embodied in the profile represent those of innocent passengers, and consider the fact that the Drug Enforcement Administration has based the profile on patterns of behavior displayed by those known to transport drugs via this country's airlines. Only then will the drug courier profile enable law enforcement officials to protect the innocent from the scourge of narcotics use and drug-related violence.

Source: Brian A. Wilson, "The War on Drugs: Evening the Odds through Use of the Airport Drug Courier Profile," 6 *Boston University Public Interest Law Journal* 203, 242 (1996).

It merely identifies common characteristics of people who traffic in illegal narcotics—irrespective of race, gender, ethnicity, or other personal immutable characteristics.

"Drug courier profiles are greatly misunderstood," another legal commentator writes.

> Once coined, a phrase too often seems to take on monolithic proportions as to its meaning. . . . Allowing trained police officers to add up apparently innocent behaviors and physical attributes to reach a reasonable suspicion of criminal activity does not constitute an overbearing intrusion on personal freedoms.[15]

Summary

The problem of illegal drugs continues to wreak devastation upon the country (and the world). Because illegal drug traffic destroys lives, families, and communities, law enforcement agents need the ability and authority to do their jobs and combat this phenomenon using the best tools at their disposal. In the 1970s, a group of dedicated agents developed a set of criteria based on years of experience, close observation, and interviews of drug couriers and drug dealers themselves. This was the "drug courier profile." Contrary to what critics may suggest, the profile is not a mask to camouflage racial discrimination. People are not profiled because they are a particular race; rather they are profiled because they fit the criteria of those who transport illegal drugs.

The Drug Courier Profile Leads to Racial Discrimination

A young African-American man hurries into the airport, needing to catch a flight home at the last minute. He purchases a ticket with cash, since he works as a waiter and his main income comes from tips. He travels to a large city that has a drug problem because that is where his parents live. He appears nervous because he has just been told that his father is gravely ill. He carries little luggage because he only heard about his father's health problem earlier that day. He used public transportation to the airport, because his car was not working properly. Sadly, this young man—who is in the midst of a family emergency—fits many of the characteristics of the malleable drug courier profile, even though he has engaged in no criminal conduct. The even sadder fact is that this young man, because he is a racial minority, is more likely to be stopped by drug enforcement agents because of this profile. While this may seem far-fetched to some who have never been profiled, it is a stark reality for many minorities in the United States. Professor Katheryn Russell-Brown writes in her book *The Color of Crime*: "Citizens who do not face the daily threat of being detained largely because of their race are unable to appreciate just how burdensome these stops can be: they become a heavy weight."[1]

Robert Wilkins, an African-American lawyer, knows first-hand the burdens of racial profiling from an incident that occurred to him in the early 1990s. He was riding in a rented Cadillac driven by his cousin on an interstate near Cumberland, Maryland. A police officer pulled over the vehicle, believing that it fit the profile of a car driven by a drug trafficker. Wilkins, who obtained his law degree from Harvard and worked in Washington, D.C., knew something was wrong. He could tell this was no ordinary traffic stop. The police ordered Wilkins and his cousin out of the car, searched the car with a narcotics dog, and finally let the two men go nearly an hour later with a $105 traffic ticket. Wilkins later sued the state police for unlawful racial profiling in *Wilkins v. Maryland State Police*. During discovery—the process in a case in which each side obtains information from the other—Wilkins's lawyers uncovered a memo stating that "drug couriers were likely to be black males and females."[2]

"There is no compensation for the type of humiliation and degradation you feel when for no other reason than the color of your skin . . . you're charged and placed in a category of drug trafficker," Wilkins said.[3] The case was eventually settled. As part of the settlement, law enforcement in Maryland had to compile data on traffic stops to determine whether race played a role in such activities. Unfortunately, the reality is that the drug courier profile often degenerates into an excuse to stop minorities for little cause, whether they are in an airport terminal, driving a car, or walking down the street.

Numerous studies have shown that black and Latino drivers, for example, are stopped far more frequently by police

Racial profile policy not well

A new federal policy that bans racial profiling is being criticized by advocacy groups for minorities as not being tough enough to end the practice.

Guidelines DO . . .

☑ Allow border security officers to consider race in preventing threats to national security

☑ Prohibit law enforcement officers from using race in routine activities, such as traffic stops

Guidelines DON'T . . .

☒ Require agency to monitor their own compliance

☒ Require collection of data on who is being stopped and why

☒ Apply to state or local officials, only federal authorities

☒ Ban religious and national-origin profiling

SOURCE: Department of Justice   AP

New guidelines for racial profiling were enacted by the federal government in 2003. Although the Justice Department issued these guidelines in order to end racial profiling by authorities in routine police work, such as drug trafficking, they do allow for the use of ethnicity and race to identify suspected terrorists.

officers than white drivers. Black and Latino drivers are more often searched than their white counterparts.[4] A study of law enforcement cameras in police cars in Volusia County, Florida, showed that 70 percent of all stopped drivers were black or Latino. Perhaps even more damning, the videotapes showed that the sheriff deputies detained minorities on average twice as long as white drivers.[5]

A proper drug courier profile does not mention race.

A federal appeals court quoted approvingly from the testimony of a respected DEA agent about the "primary" characteristics of drug couriers. These included:

(1) arrival from or departure to an identified source city; (2) carrying little or no luggage, or large quantities of empty suitcases; (3) unusual itinerary, such as rapid turnaround time for a very lengthy airplane trip; (4) use of an alias; (5) carrying unusually large amounts of currency in the many thousands of dollars, usually on their person, in briefcases or bags; (6) purchasing airline tickets with a large amount of small denomination currency; and (7) unusual nervousness beyond that ordinarily exhibited by passenger.[6]

The DEA agent described the "secondary" characteristics of the profile as:

(1) the almost exclusive use of public transportation, particularly taxicabs, in departing from the airport; (2) immediately making a telephone call after deplaning; (3) leaving a false or fictitious call-back telephone number with the airline being utilized; and (4) excessively frequent travel to source or distribution cities.[7]

The problem with the characteristics in this drug courier profile is that much of the supposed suspicious activity can indicate quite innocent conduct. Millions of people live in large cities that may be characterized as a drug source city. Some people may not have a credit card as a result of personal choice or past financial difficulty. Should this place them under a cloud of suspicion?

The drug courier profile often criminalizes innocent behavior.

Judge George C. Pratt of the U.S. Court of Appeals for the Second Circuit called the drug courier profile "laughable" because of the way it could be manipulated and changed by agents to fit whatever situation they desired. He wrote: "The 'drug courier profile' . . . is so fluid that it can be used to justify designating anyone a potential drug courier if the DEA agents so choose."[8] Pratt listed the following as some of the characteristics identified by various DEA agents in different cases as part of the profile: arriving late at night; arriving early in the morning; first to deplane; last to deplane; deplaned in the middle; used a one-way ticket; used a round-trip ticket; carried brand-new luggage; carried a gym bag; traveled alone; traveled with a

QUOTABLE

Testimony of DEA Agent Paul Markonni

Basically, it's a number of characteristics which we attribute or which we believe can be used to pick out drug couriers. And these characteristics are basically things that normal travelers do not do, and, in other words, you may have one characteristic that will apply to someone, but not a number of them. These are things that even the ticket agents and airline personnel believe to be suspicious and they are, basically, obvious nervousness. An individual taking a trip to a far-away city with very little or no luggage, and, to us, specifically, the cities of Los Angeles and San Diego and some of the Texas border areas where narcotics are distributed—the most significant heroin distribution area in the United States right now.

Individuals who will fly under assumed names. Individuals who will give false or fictitious call back telephone numbers to the airlines. Individuals who travel with large amounts of currency, and this is noted by . . . either the ticket agent or the airport security people during routine searches of baggage. Individuals who will deplane and make a telephone call directly after or immediately after deplaning. This, again, is not one of the most significant characteristics but yet it holds true in most of the cases that we have encountered. Basically a courier is a person travelling alone, a person who generally will not have anyone meet him or her at the airport. In the majority of cases the courier has been a black female.

Source: *United States v. McClain*, 452 F.Supp. 195, 1999 (E.D. Mich. 1977).

companion; acted too nervous; acted too calm; wore expensive clothing and gold jewelry; dressed in black corduroys; white pullover shirt; wore loafers without socks; dressed in dark slacks, work shirt, and hat; dressed in brown leather aviator jacket, gold chain, hair down to shoulders; dressed in loose-fitting sweatshirt and denim jacket; walked rapidly through airport; walked aimlessly through the airport; and had a white handkerchief in his hand.[9]

Drug courier profiles often have a race-based component.

Such drug courier profiles fall heavily upon racial minorities. Police officers have used the profile as a mask to pull over members of particular racial groups with far greater frequency than whites. Judge Richard Arnold of the U.S. Court of Appeals for the Eighth Circuit warned about the use of race in applying drug courier profile characteristics: "Use of race as a factor simply reinforces the kind of stereotyping that lies behind drug-courier profiles. When public officials begin to regard large groups of citizens as presumptively criminal, this country is in a perilous situation indeed."[10]

If law enforcement officials use race as the primary basis for stopping a citizen, they may violate the Equal Protection Clause of the Fourteenth Amendment, which states that government officials must treat similarly situated individuals equally. The Equal Protection Clause provides that the government must not "deny to any person within its jurisdiction the equal protection of the laws." Judge Nathaniel Jones of the U.S. Court of Appeals for the Sixth Circuit explained in a drug courier case:

A person cannot become the target of a police investigation solely on the basis of skin color. Such selective law enforcement is forbidden. . . . If law enforcement adopts a policy, employs a practice, or in a given situation takes steps to initiate an investigation of a citizen based solely upon that citizen's race, without more, then a violation of the Equal Protection Clause has occurred.[11]

Moreover, the use of the drug courier profile not only violates the Equal Protection Clause, it often violates the Fourth Amendment, which prohibits government officials from engaging in unreasonable searches and seizures.

FROM THE BENCH

State v. Williams, 525 N.W.2d 538, 548 (Minn. 1995)

In the case of *State v. Williams*, the Minnesota Supreme Court criticized the drug courier profile in its ruling, which read in part:

> This is not to say that a reasonable and prudent police officer or DEA agent is not free to keep a mental checklist of possibly relevant factors bearing on their important role in intercepting drug couriers. It is simply to say that drug courier profiles are not "scientific" in any sense of the word, that agents may not mechanically rely on them in making investigative decisions affecting the constitutional privacy interests of citizens, and that reviewing courts also must not engage in a mechanistic deference to police testimony that the defendant's conduct fit some profile. Rather, reviewing courts must instead focus on the totality of all the relevant circumstances bearing upon the propriety of the officer's conduct. . . .
>
> We believe, however, that the evidence admitted in this case is clearly and plainly inadmissible. Basically, what the officers testified was that in their experience most drug couriers behave a certain way—*e.g.*, buy their tickets with cash, typically come from a so-called "source" city such as Detroit, typically use the club car on the train, etc.—and the jury was impliedly urged to infer that since defendant's conduct fit the profile, she must have known that her luggage contained crack cocaine. Admitting evidence of this sort is very similar to admitting evidence that a defendant in a child abuse case was abused as a child and that child abusers typically were abused as children.

The use of drug courier profile testimony in court is wrong.

Sometimes prosecutors at drug trials seek to persuade a jury and prove a defendant's guilt by claiming that he or she fits this malleable profile. Such convictions, however, have been overturned upon appeal. The Minnesota Supreme Court, for example, reversed a defendant's conviction for drug possession in part because the prosecutor claimed that the defendant, an African-American woman, fit a drug courier profile. The woman had claimed that she did not have knowledge of drugs that were found in one of her bags. The court bluntly suggested that race is often a factor in drug courier profile cases: "One does not have to be a cynic to believe that, despite protestations to the contrary, a key but unarticulated and, perhaps, unrecognized factor in many cases is that the person's skin is, to use the words of Rodgers and Hammerstein, 'of a different shade.'"[12]

Law professor Mark Kadish explains that courts should be very hesitant about allowing prosecutors to introduce testimony about a drug courier profile into a criminal trial. At times, prosecutors have introduced evidence suggesting that a defendant fit a profile before the defendant's attorneys can establish their client's character. Under the law of evidence, the prosecution generally cannot introduce character evidence about a defendant until the defendant first introduces the fact that he or she possesses good character.

Summary

The use of racial profiling in both the drug courier profile and in the war on drugs in general imposes terrible costs on society. It creates great distrust within minorities across the United States, as they become reluctant to trust the police and to give them needed information that could help improve the quality of life in their communities. Many blacks and Latinos, both citizens and non-citizens, come to view the police as an enemy or, at the very least, not a friend. Without the support of the community, law enforcement officials solve fewer crimes. Community-based policing is the preferred model for law enforcement. As law professor Kevin Johnson writes: "It is not possible to effectively combat crime without cooperation from minority communities."[13] Those groups who are subjected to racial profiling resent the police conduct. It creates questioning of the legitimacy and fairness of the criminal justice system. Furthermore, as author David Harris concludes: "Racial profiling is neither an efficient nor an effective tool for fighting crime."[14]

Some Racial Profiling Is Necessary in the War on Terror

On September 11, 2001, 19 men perpetrated horrific acts of terrorism that culminated in the deaths of nearly 3,000 people in New York City, outside Washington, D.C., and in a field in Pennsylvania. These 19 men hijacked and crashed four commercial airliners, destroying them along with the entire World Trade Center in New York and severely damaging the Pentagon outside Washington. All of these men were 20 to 40 years old, all were of Arab or Middle Eastern descent, and all believed in a radical Islamic fundamentalism preached by Osama bin Laden, head of the al Qaeda terrorist network, which has declared war on America and has threatened more terrorist actions.

Two of the 9/11 terrorists, Mohamed Atta and Abdulaziz al-Omari, were easily able to board a plane heading out of Portland, Maine, on the morning of September 11, to Boston, Massachusetts. When Atta checked in for his flight in Boston, a computer program known as the Computer Assisted Passenger Prescreening System (CAPPS) identified him as a "person of interest." The only result was that Atta's bags were not placed on the airplane until he boarded the plane. This occurred as a precaution in case Atta was a terrorist who had placed a bomb in his baggage that would go off. The use of CAPPS, however, did not stop Atta from boarding the plane and completing his mission as a suicide bomber.[1] Fellow 9/11 terrorists Satam al Suqami, Wail al Shahri, and Waleed al Shehri were also flagged by CAPPS when they boarded planes headed to Los Angeles. In fact, while CAPPS flagged more than half of the 19 terrorists involved in the attacks, the computer system did not prevent a single terrorist from boarding the planes.[2]

For those who lived through the events of 9/11, it remains baffling that law enforcement officials did not pull any of these 19 terrorists off their planes. After all, September 11 was not the first time that radical Islamic extremists had tried to kill Americans and destroy symbols of the nation's military and economic power. In February 1993, Muslim extremists bombed the World Trade Center in New York City. Fortunately, the attack—which involved a car bomb in a subterranean parking garage—did not come off as intended, though it did kill six people and wounded 1,000 more. More recently, in November 2009, another alleged Islamic extremist, Nidal Malik Hasan, who was a major in the U.S. Army, opened fire on fellow soldiers, killing 13 people. Hasan yelled out *Allahu Akbar* ("God is Great") as he fired. Associates recalled that Hasan had equated the war on terrorism with a war against the religion of Islam. He also apparently attended a mosque in Virginia led by a radical Islamist religious leader and expressed sympathy for suicide bombers.[3]

If better profiling practices had been implemented, some or all of these terrorist attacks might have been prevented. Profiling can work. Consider that an alert airport official stopped Mohammad al-Qatani, the would-be twentieth 9/11 terrorist, in Orlando, Florida. That airport official profiled

Two men, indentified by authorities as suspected 9/11 hijackers *(from right)* Mohamed Atta and Abdulaziz al-Omari, pass through airport security at Portland International Jetport on September 11, 2001. Authorities say the two men took a commuter flight to Boston before boarding American Airlines Flight 11, one of the two jetliners that was flown into the World Trade Center in New York City.

al-Qatani and, thus, prevented him from joining his terrorist colleagues, leading to his detainment.[4] Certainly, profiling may be abused if used indiscriminately and without proper oversight. To avoid profiling entirely, however, is not only bad policy, it is dangerous to national security.

Profiling is necessary to fight the war on terror.

Leaders of the free world must recognize the harsh reality that there are radical Islamists who wish to destroy the Western world. They will use any means necessary—including acts of mass murder—to achieve their insidious objectives. They view the Western world, particularly the United States, as a great evil or, as they sometimes say, "the Great Satan," because they see our plurality, tolerance, and democratic principles as contrary to the violent brand of Islam to which they adhere. They believe it is their duty to engage in horrific acts of terrorism and kill innocent civilians. They have proven time and time again that they will kill innocent Americans and others to further their goals. Creating a terrorist profile that takes into account whether someone is Middle Eastern or Muslim is simply good common sense, not racial or religious discrimination.

Newt Gingrich, the former speaker of the U.S. House of Representatives and current political commentator and author, writes that "the scale, persistence and sophistication of the enemy requires an honesty, a clarity and a scale appropriate to the response."[5] He adds that "it is time to know more about would-be terrorists, to profile for terrorists and to actively discriminate based on suspicious terrorist information."[6]

We should not worry about political correctness.

It may be discomforting to some, but the reality is that many of the world's terrorists are radical Muslim extremists of Middle Eastern descent. Unfortunately, many political leaders and the nation's major media outlets often fail to investigate thoroughly enough the dangers of radical Islam. Fearing that they may be accused of discrimination, they ignore the dangers of Muslim extremists and fail to explain the threat they pose to U.S. citizens. This is the essence of political correctness. More must be done to inform the American public about the threat that radical Islam poses to this country and to the world.[7]

In July 2001, just two months before the 9/11 attacks, FBI agent Kenneth Williams wrote a memo about the possibility of Muslim extremists engaging in airplane training at flight schools in Arizona. He suggested that the FBI commit greater resources

Legislative Proposal in New York—Terrorist Profile

After the 9/11 terrorist attacks, members of the New York State Legislature proposed a bill to use ethnic profiling to thwart future terrorist attacks. The following is an excerpt from the proposed legislation:

> The legislature finds and declares that preventing terrorist attacks on our citizens—including not only possible deaths and injuries, but also crushing economic harm or even chaos—is an even more compelling governmental interest. It also finds and declares that since both law enforcement resources and the time necessary to make an initial decision regarding stopping and questioning are very limited, this compelling governmental interest demands the identification of potential terrorist suspects as effectively and efficiently as possible so that they may be stopped, questioned, frisked and/or searched.
>
> The legislature also finds and declares that experts have suggested that, while no one single factor is definitive, a wide variety of factors such as the following can help identify potential terrorism suspects: wearing heavy clothing in warm weather; carrying a briefcase, duffle bag or backpack with protrusions or visible wires; displaying nervousness and/or inappropriate sweating; an inability or unwillingness to make eye contact; chemical burns on clothing or stains on hands. For this reason, law enforcement personnel are often asked to look for and consider such factors in determining which persons to stop, question, frisk and/or search.
>
> The legislature also finds and declares that, as many experts and also the history of modern terrorism has suggested, the race or ethnicity of a person can also be a very important if not crucial factor, along with others, in identifying potential terrorist suspects, and so finds that the use of race or ethnicity serves a compelling governmental interest in helping law enforcement personnel to determine effectively and efficiently, along with other factors, which persons to stop, question, frisk and/or search. . . .
>
> Notwithstanding any state or local law, rule or regulation to the contrary, a peace officer or police officer . . . may consider the apparent race or ethnicity of a suspect as one of many factors in a potential terrorist suspect profile which he or she could use to identify persons who could be stopped, questioned, frisked and/or searched in furtherance of the government's compelling interest in deterring terrorist attacks.

Source: http://open.nysenate.gov/legislation/bill/S6690.

to uncovering potential terrorist plots by Muslim men in the terrorist group al Qaeda using airplanes. His eight-page memo explained that he and other agents in Phoenix had observed a number of young Muslim men attending flight schools in the area. The memo urged the FBI to commit greater resources to explore the possibility that Osama bin Laden was sending young Muslim men here to flight schools to later use airplanes in terrorist attacks.[8]

His memo was ignored because some feared that Williams's plan would be perceived as discriminatory. Michelle Malkin writes: "If the FBI had taken Williams' advice, the feelings of some Arabs and Muslims might have been hurt. But the Twin Towers might still be standing and 3,000 innocent people might be alive today."[9]

Protecting civil liberties is not as important as protecting American lives.

Civil liberties are precious. They distinguish the United States from many other countries around the globe. But terrorists have used our open society against us, entering our country and plotting to kill us. The primary responsibility of the American government is to provide security for its people. We cannot enjoy civil liberties if Muslim extremists have murdered us. This requires the government to be given a freer hand to deal with the terrorist threat.

"Profiling is not about bigotry," said Mark Flanagan, a former state legislator from Florida. "It's about history, it's about evidence. It's about common sense. Terrorists are changing their tactics constantly, and they're taking advantage of our failure not to profile."[10]

The public supports some form of profiling.

We live in a constitutional democracy that supports the principle of majority rule and popular sovereignty. This means that the public has a strong say in what happens in this country. The public supports the profiling of would-be terrorists to ensure that another major attack like 9/11 does not occur. Commentator Sharon R. Reddick reports: "Before the tragic events of that day [on September 11, 2001], eighty percent of Americans opposed racial profiling. Today, sixty percent of Americans believe in the necessity of some form of profiling to ensure public safety and national security."[11]

After the attempted bombing on December 25, 2009, of an airplane by a Muslim passenger from Nigeria, Rasmussen conducted another poll on racial profiling: 59 percent of the public believed that race and ethnicity should be taken into account

QUOTABLE

Editorial Supporting Some Use of Profiling

Authorities don't need to search every passenger for 100 ml of hand lotion just because a cadre of Islamic extremists in Britain planned to use sports drinks and toothpaste to blow up as many as 10 jetliners simultaneously in 2006. They don't need to have every elderly lady take off her shoes for X-raying, either, or have every rotund Caucasian male remove his belt and hobble through the metal detector with one hand on his waistband.

What is needed is profiling of passengers—their behaviour, travel history, sex, ethnicity, travel-companion status and outward religious aspect. Men are far more likely to be terrorists than women, so men should receive greater scrutiny. Young adults are more likely to be terrorists than the aged. Religious Muslims who've travelled frequently to Yemen or Nigeria or Pakistan are statistically more likely to be terrorists than Sikhs, nuns and Quakers. Men travelling alone are more likely to be terrorists than men travelling with their children. No one should be treated as a presumptive terrorist. But only the willfully blind can ignore the fact that almost the entire terrorist threat originates with a small subset of the travelling population.

The federal government's announcement on Tuesday that it will step up security for flights going from Canada to the United States was a mixed effort, then. On the one hand, it again focuses on interdicting dangerous objects, which is hit-and-miss at best. But it does, for the first time, also acknowledge that more profiling is necessary.

Source: *National Post* (Canada), January 7, 2010, p. A12.

by officials at airports before determining whom to search. The poll also showed that more than 70 percent supported profiling in general.[12] Interestingly, in November 2009, just prior to that attempted bombing but after the Fort Hood massacre, more than 60 percent surveyed believed that political correctness prevented the military from responding to warning signs from Hasan at Fort Hood. "Profiling is certainly not the be-all, end-all of national security and counterterror protocol," Jeff P. Emanuel writes. "After all, it is easy to list terrorists who have either been non-Muslim or non-Middle Eastern. However, for every individual resembling Richard Reid, Timothy McVeigh, Eric Rudolph, or Jose Padilla, . . . there are exponentially more terrorists of Middle Eastern descent."[13] Rachel Ehrenfeld, author of *Funding Evil: How Terrorism Is Financed—and How to Stop It*, explains that profiling has a long history: "Profiling has been used by law enforcement the world over for decades to identify criminals."[14]

Summary

Racial profiling is viewed as a dirty term. Critics claim that it discriminates against people based on race and ethnicity and that it harms relations between government officials and citizens. It is, however, an effective law enforcement tool, particularly in the battle for national security in the war on terrorism. If applied properly, it results not in racial discrimination but in rational discrimination.

Muslim extremists have declared war on America, conducted terrorist attacks on U.S. embassies abroad, and committed heinous attacks on American soil, culminating in the horror of September 11, 2001. Osama bin Laden and others of his ilk will stop at nothing to perpetrate another major terrorist attack on American soil. National security should be the foremost concern of government officials. We cannot enjoy civil liberties if terrorists kill us.

Government officials and citizens alike must understand that many terrorists in the world do fit a certain profile—they are from the Middle East and subscribe to a radical form of Islam. These extremists are dangerous and we must do everything we can to protect the public from their nefarious intentions. One way to combat these terrorists is through a terrorist profile, which would allow officials to consider race, ethnicity, and religion in conducting assessments. Moreover, the American public strongly supports some form of profiling by race and ethnicity to protect our country. Particularly after the events of 9/11, politicians, law enforcement officers, and national security officials must not let political correctness trump survival. As columnist Kathleen Parker wrote shortly after 9/11: "A terrorist attack of such enormous proportions ... makes racial profiling a temporary necessity that no patriotic American should protest."[15]

Racial Profiling in the War on Terror Is Wrong and Costly

A couple of months after the terrorist attacks of September 11, 2001, a woman was detained at a Chicago airport. She was intending to travel to Tel Aviv, Israel, to visit her ailing father. Instead, she believed she was singled out for very intensive security screening. She protested what she believed to be profiling in the wake of 9/11. Chicago police then charged her with disorderly conduct, and she had to spend two days in jail. As a result of the racial profiling, Anna Mustafa lost the chance to see her father one last time before he died. She was no terrorist. She was a responsible citizen who once served on the Chicago Board of Education. Describing the event a few years later, she said: "No one should have to go through this nightmare. I lost my job, my reputation, and the chance to say any last words to my father. . . . I am an American citizen. Arab Americans are part of the social structure of this country."[1]

The tale of Anna Mustafa is not unique. A few weeks after 9/11, Ali Erikenoglu heard a knock on his door in Paterson, New Jersey. Four agents from the Federal Bureau of Investigation (FBI) entered his home, questioned his patriotism, and rummaged through his belongings. He had to produce his Social Security number, phone numbers, work address, level of education, passport, and the names of several friends. "What kind of American are you?" one agent asked the American-born Muslim. The agents warned Erikenoglu that, if he had made any phone calls to terrorists, they would return to his home, handcuff him, and take him to jail. "I was terrified," he recalled.[2]

Consider also the plight of Mohammed Ali of Denton, Texas. Police officers pulled over his vehicle, allegedly because one of his car lights was brighter than the other. The officers then asked him a number of times whether he had any dead bodies or bombs in his vehicle. The officers searched his car without his consent. They found a small pocketknife on the passenger side of his vehicle and arrested him. His case was later dropped in court, but he did not file a complaint against the Sanger Police Department because he feared that such a complaint might lead to further harassment or retaliation.[3]

Unfortunately, such tales of racial profiling are common in the post-9/11 era. There has been widespread profiling of Arab Americans and of people of Arab or Middle Eastern descent living in the United States. Dr. Riad Z. Abdelkarim probably spoke for many when he wrote: "Ever since the terrorist attacks against the U.S. of Sept. 11, 2001, we have had our loyalty to our country challenged, our patriotism questioned, our institutions raided, and our civil liberties stomped upon."[4] An Arab-American newspaper referred to this phenomenon as "Islamophobia."[5] The Council on American-Islamic Relations warned: "When 9-11 happened, the people already predisposed to viewing Islam with suspicion jumped on this bandwagon and through a multitude of primarily right wing outlets have been successful in creating a climate of extreme prejudice, suspicion and fear against Muslims."[6]

Federal programs after 9/11 profiled Arabs and Middle Easterners.

After 9/11, if you were a young Arab, Middle Easterner, or Muslim living in the United States, you became a suspect, regardless of whether you were a citizen or not. It became a scary time of guilt by association. You could be questioned by the FBI, targeted by immigration officials, and interrogated for hours by immigration officials. Attorney General John Ashcroft instituted a policy that led to mass questioning of thousands of young Arab, Middle Eastern, and Muslim men. The men were questioned about their feelings on the September 11 attacks, their possible involvement in terrorism, whether they knew anyone who had guns or explosives, and whether they had any weapons training.[7] Although the government claimed that it obtained valuable information, no terrorism arrests were made.[8] It appears that the government expended tremendous amounts of resources, targeting a specific community with no positive results.

Ashcroft also instituted another program called the National Security Entry-Exit Registration System, or NSEERS. It required thousands of young people from Middle Eastern countries to go to federal immigration headquarters to answer questions and to prove that they were legally in the United States. Young men from 25 countries with ties to known terrorist organizations had to register with law enforcement officials. The men were fingerprinted, photographed, and subjected to interrogations. One aspect of the program was a domestic component that solicited registrations from 80,000 individuals in the United States on temporary visas.[9] This program devastated many families. Amnesty International reports: "Shortly after NSEERS was enacted, affected communities around the U.S. lost large portions of their male population, resulting in the rapid impoverishment and destabilization of many families."[10]

The obsession with ferreting out terrorists, while a laudable objective, has unfortunately led to widespread profiling. In 2002, federal immigration officials deported 75 percent more undocumented Arabs and Muslims than they did in 2001. The *Philadelphia Inquirer* reported, "The ethnic makeup of deported foreigners shows how far immigration-enforcement officials went to tailor their focus by nationality after the September 11 attacks."[11]

NSEERS was only perhaps the most visible evidence of mass profiling of citizens and noncitizens of Arab or Middle Eastern descent. Other actions by law enforcement officials were also questionable. The FBI ordered its field supervisors to count the number of mosques and Muslims in their areas for counterterrorism purposes.[12]

Terrorists may come from anywhere and everywhere.

The problem with a myopic obsession with people who hail from Middle Eastern countries is that terrorism can come from anywhere and anybody, regardless of racial or ethnic background, can be a terrorist. Timothy McVeigh, who carried out

QUOTABLE

ACLU on NSEERS Program

More than seven years after its implementation, NSEERS continues to impact the lives of those individuals and communities subjected to it. It has led to the prevention of naturalization and to the deportation of individuals who failed to register, either because they were unaware of the registration requirement or because they were afraid to register after hearing stories of interrogations, detentions, and deportations of friends, family, and community members. As a result, well-intentioned individuals who failed to comply with NSEERS due to a lack of knowledge or fear have been denied "adjustment of status" (green cards), and in some cases have been placed in removal proceedings for "willfully" failing to register.

Source: "The Persistence of Racial and Ethnic Profiling in the United States," ACLU, August 2009, p. 30, http://www.aclu.org/files/pdfs/humanrights/cerd_finalreport.pdf.

the horrific bombing of a federal building in Oklahoma City in 1995, was an American-born white man who had earned a medal in the United States armed forces during the 1990–1991 Persian Gulf War. In 1962, a 34-year-old Caucasian man named Thomas Doty carried out the first successful sabotage of a commercial jet. In 1994, an off-duty FedEx employee named Auburn Calloway nearly succeeded in skyjacking an airplane and crashing it into FedEx headquarters.

Other terrorists have not fit the profile of an Arab from the Middle East. Richard Reid, the so-called shoe bomber, is half-West Indian with a British passport. José Padilla, the so-called dirty bomber, is a Hispanic American. Zacarias Moussaoui is an African man with a French passport. John Walker Lindh, the "American Taliban," is white. None of them fit the profile yet were avowed terrorists who committed or tried to commit terrorist acts against the United States.[13]

There is another danger in assuming that all major terrorist attacks are committed by people of Arab or Middle Eastern descent—it allows the real terrorists to escape detection for long periods of time. Timothy McVeigh escaped detention for a time because law enforcement officials assumed that "Arab terrorists" had committed the attack on the federal building in Oklahoma City.[14] "When we construct a profile using the wrong kind of characteristic—a racial or an ethnic one as opposed to markers of behavior—we spread our enforcement resources and efforts more thinly than we would otherwise," David Harris writes.[15]

Profiling creates distrust in the Muslim community.

Racial profiling of Arab nationals and Arab Americans creates great distrust in the American Muslim community. This is problematic because members of that community may provide the best information on potential terrorist plots that they might hear rumors about. Because only a small segment of the Muslim community is likely involved with or in support of violence, it is counterproductive and dangerous to alienate the vast majority of the population who do not support the violence with misguided profiling policies. Professors Deborah Ramirez and Stephanie Woldenberg write that racial profiling of Arabs and Muslims "succeeds only in alienating one of the most important, substantial, and untapped resources for intelligence."[16] They describe this untapped resource as "the linguistic and cultural expertise that the Arab and Muslim communities can bring to the table with law enforcement in a joint effort to prevent future acts of terrorism."[17] Another legal commentator writes: "Ending the use of selective enforcement against certain communities can also help restore dialogue with immigrant communities, which have proven to be key allies in the war on terrorism."[18]

The social costs of racial profiling are extreme. It leads to "distressed individuals, disconnected communities, and diminished domestic security capabilities."[19] Those individuals who are victims of racial profiling, including Arab Americans who have been loyal citizens their entire lives, live in a state of paralyzing fear. Some do not even want to travel for fear of harassment from law enforcement officials. That is clearly not the way a free society is supposed to operate. Adult victims of profiling say that the distress is manifold when witnessed by young children. One man said that his young daughter now cries every time she sees a police officer.[20]

Even worse, it may lead some Arab Americans or Arab or Middle Eastern immigrants to be much more reluctant to help the police in their counterterrorism efforts. One legal commentator explains that "the cooperation of immigrant communities where 'sleeper cells' may be hiding has been critical in disrupting terrorist plots in America and abroad."[21] U.S. citizens of Arab descent have provided key information to foil potential terrorist plots in Buffalo, New York, and other locations nationwide. Deputy Attorney General Larry Thompson stressed that Muslim Americans were important in the detection of five suspected al Qaeda operatives in Lackawanna, New York. He said that "the assistance of Muslim Americans in this case has helped to make the Buffalo community and our nation safer."[22]

Racial profiling leads to a rise in hate crimes.

Such over-profiling not only presents a security risk by alienating a key segment of the community, but it also has another harmful side effect. It leads to a pattern of hate crimes against Arabs and Muslims—anyone somehow believed by their attackers to be associated with 9/11 terrorists. Less than a year after 9/11, the Council on American-Islamic Relations reported that at least 1,700 anti-Muslim incidents had occurred. "Since many of them go unreported, the actual number is likely much higher."[23]

The level of vehemence against Americans and nationals of Arab or Middle Eastern descent reached shocking levels at times. In Chicago, Illinois, a group of hundreds of people gathered near a high school. A few engaged in a threatening chant: "Kill the Arabs!" In Cleveland, Ohio, a man drove his car through the front entrance of a local mosque. In Houston, Texas, an Islamic school had to close for fear of violence.[24]

Civilrights.org reports that hate crimes against Arabs, Muslims, and Sikhs (who are neither Arab nor Muslim) living in the United States increased dramatically after 9/11. The group determined that the number of hate crimes in 2001 was 17 times greater than in the previous year. Not only that, the group also said that the problem remained even years after 9/11: "While the number of reported hate crimes against Arab Americans, Muslims, and Sikhs has declined from the peak of 2001, it remains substantially above pre-2001 levels. In 2007, for example, 115 hate crimes were reported—more than four times as many as were reported in 2000."[25]

Summary

The United States changed in many ways after the horrible terrorist attacks of September 11, 2001. The country made some improvements in airport security and instituted other needed security measures. Unfortunately, another result of the attacks was widespread profiling of citizens and noncitizens of Arab and Middle Eastern descent at the federal, state, and local levels. Federal programs led to the mass questioning and even detention of young Arab and Middle Eastern citizens and nationals across the country. Other programs led to the deportation and detention of many Arab and Middle Eastern immigrants, the vast majority of whom had no connection to any type of terrorism or terrorists. It was classic guilt by association.

Terrorists come in all shapes and sizes, all races and religions. Focusing on people of Middle Eastern descent and Arabic appearance is not a good proxy for detecting criminal behavior. It is a lazy law enforcement practice that actually harms security. It harms security in part because it alienates a key segment of the population who may actually be able to help in many circumstances. Profiling these innocent groups of people is also harmful because it leads to a rise in hate crimes and other forms of societal discrimination. This is un-American.

Some Racial Profiling Is Necessary to Combat Illegal Immigration

I n March 2007, Tessa Tranchant and her friend Allison Kunhardt were sitting in a car at an intersection in Virginia Beach, Virginia, waiting for the red light to turn green. Both young women wore their seat belts. As the light turned green, they proceeded into the intersection. But suddenly, a car traveling at more than 70 miles per hour crashed into them, killing them instantly. The driver of the car, Alfredo Ramos, was intoxicated and did not see the red light or the car in the intersection. Oblivious to anything, Ramos took two innocent lives.

Twice before, Ramos had been convicted of drunken driving offenses and public intoxication. He also had a fake driver's license and could not speak English. Ramos was an illegal immigrant who should have been deported after a previous criminal offense. Instead, he was allowed to stay in this country and take innocent lives. As Tessa's father, Ray, testified before Congress:

"Ramos pays nothing, has no driver's training, no insurance, no lawyer, no license, and now the American people have to spend approximately $30,000 a year for 40 years to rehabilitate—then deport him. The taxpayers have to pay for it."[1] Ray Tranchant testified that he was not insensitive to the issue of racial profiling, but he made the following point: "A family should not have to mourn the death of a loved one just because of an unrelated policy or the political correctness of not offending or inconveniencing a few people. This prevents us from making our communities safer, a constitutional right to all citizens of the United States."[2]

Sadly, Tessa Tranchant and Allison Kunhardt are not the only innocent victims of crimes perpetrated by illegal immigrants. Illegal aliens commit a high proportion of crimes in the United States, many people believe. For this reason U.S. Representative Walter Jones from North Carolina has, beginning in 2008, introduced legislation called the Illegal Alien Crime Reporting Act that would require states to compile statistics of crimes committed by illegal immigrants. "Crimes committed by illegal aliens are plaguing cities and states across our nation," Congressman Jones said.[3]

The use of race is an important tool in border and immigration matters.

The U.S. Supreme Court has ruled that race may be used as a factor in determining whether or not a person is an illegal immigrant and subject to further search and possible deportation. In *United States v. Brignoni-Ponce* (1975), the Court wrote: "The likelihood that any given person of Mexican ancestry is an alien is high enough to make a Mexican appearance a relevant factor, but standing alone it does not justify stopping all Mexican-Americans to ask if they are aliens."[4] This ruling means that law enforcement and border officials can use "Mexican ancestry" (or more broadly, Latino/Hispanic appearance) as a factor in determining whether someone is in the country illegally.

The Supreme Court also determined that "when an officer's observations lead him reasonably to suspect that a particular vehicle may contain aliens who are illegally in the country, he may stop the car briefly and investigate the circumstances that provoke suspicion."[5] Other factors the Court said that officers could take into account were proximity to the border, the usual patterns of traffic on the road, previous experience with aliens in the specific location, and the irregular driving or behavior of the driver or occupants of the vehicle.[6]

More recent court decisions recognize the fact that race can be a significant factor in determining the constitutionality of searches of vehicles and people near the border. In *United States v. Aldo Antonio Hernandez-Moya* (2009), the U.S. Court

FROM THE BENCH

United States v. Brignoni-Ponce, 422 U.S. 873, 885-887 (1975)

Any number of factors may be taken into account in deciding whether there is reasonable suspicion to stop a car in the border area. Officers may consider the characteristics of the area in which they encounter a vehicle. Its proximity to the border, the usual patterns of traffic on the particular road, and previous experience with alien traffic are all relevant. They also may consider information about recent illegal border crossings in the area. The driver's behavior may be relevant, as erratic driving or obvious attempts to evade officers can support a reasonable suspicion. Aspects of the vehicle itself may justify suspicion. For instance, officers say that certain station wagons, with large compartments for fold-down seats or spare tires, are frequently used for transporting concealed aliens. The vehicle may appear to be heavily loaded, it may have an extraordinary number of passengers, or the officers may observe persons trying to hide. The Government also points out that trained officers can recognize the characteristic appearance of persons who live in Mexico, relying on such factors as the mode of dress and haircut. In all situations the officer is entitled to assess the facts in light of his experience in detecting illegal entry and smuggling.

of Appeals for the Fifth Circuit determined that the fact that six people in a van were all of Hispanic ancestry was a relevant factor under the Supreme Court's test in *Brignoni-Ponce* that helped to uphold the validity of the search, which found that the van contained six illegal immigrants who were trying to sneak into the United States from Mexico.[7] A Border Patrol agent first noticed that the van contained six people of Hispanic appearance. When he looked at the van again, it contained only two people of Hispanic appearance. The agent inferred that the other four passengers in the backseats of the van had ducked to evade notice from the Border Patrol. "Agent Meyer also observed that the passengers appeared to be Hispanic," the Fifth Circuit Court wrote. "*Brignoni-Ponce* held that while a stop based on the ethnicity of the vehicle occupants alone cannot be justified, appearance and ethnicity can be considered as another factor."[8]

Another federal appeals court upheld a search conducted by an experienced Border Patrol agent in Florida who noticed a van with California license plates carrying six Hispanic men in an area known for immigrant smuggling. In *United States v. Bautista-Silva* (2009), the U.S. Court of Appeals for the 11th Circuit determined that the totality of the circumstances—including the multiple factors from *Brignoni-Ponce*—justified the Border Patrol agent's search of the vehicle containing several Hispanics.[9]

The reality is that the vast majority of illegal immigrants in the United States are Latinos or Hispanics, most of whom have crossed the U.S.-Mexico border. A study by the Pew Hispanic Center determined: "Unauthorized migrants from Mexico and the rest of Latin America represented 78% of the unauthorized population in 2005."[10] It is nonsensical then to suggest that law enforcement officials cannot take race into account at all. It ignores reality. "[H]ow are U.S. authorities to wage the fight against illegal immigration if they may not take race into account?" the *Chattanooga Times Free Press* asked in an editorial. "The overwhelming majority of illegal aliens in the United States are from Latin America."[11]

Agents of the U.S. Border Patrol detain illegal immigrants who were apprehended just over the Mexican border near McAllen, Texas, on May 28, 2010. During the 2009 fiscal year, more than 540,000 such immigrants were apprehended illegally entering the United States all along the southern border with Mexico.

Securing the border is vital to national security.

Concerns over racial profiling must take a backseat to racial reality. Many illegal immigrants enter this country over the porous U.S.-Mexico border. Too many of these illegal aliens come across the border and then commit crimes, critics say. The southern border also serves as a passageway for terrorists to enter the country, including members of al Qaeda. Some counterterrorism experts warn that terrorists are using the border to funnel dangerous weapons into the United States.[12]

Groups like the Federation for American Immigration Reform (FAIR) warn that the United States must step up its enforcement and protection of the borders. If not, they believe the country could be more susceptible to another major terrorist attack and increased criminal activities, including drug trafficking. Border security must be enhanced and immigration laws must be more vigorously enforced to reduce the number of illegal immigrants. Many people view the problem of a porous U.S.-Mexico border as simply a debate over social services, such as health care or education, or as a debate over fundamental fairness. It should be a debate about national security.[13]

ICE agreements with local law enforcement are necessary.

Immigration and Customs Enforcement (ICE) has the daunting task of protecting the nation and enforcing its immigration laws. In 1996, Congress passed the Illegal Immigration Reform and Immigrant Responsibility Act. A key provision of that law is Section 287(g), which enables the cooperation of local and state law enforcement officials in the immigration enforcement effort.[14]

To allow this cooperation, state and local officials must sign a formal Memorandum of Agreement (MOA). Under the MOA, local and state officials become deputized to perform the functions of immigration officers. This means that local law enforcement officers have the power to investigate immigration violations and collect evidence in the routine exercise of immigration laws. State and local officials undergo extensive training in federal immigration laws before enforcing such laws.

This 287(g) program has been vital to protecting and enforcing the nation's laws. It has allowed local and state law enforcement officials to make more than 40,000 arrests for immigration law violations. Professor Kris W. Kobach, one of the nation's leading authorities on immigration law, testified before Congress that "to curtail or eliminate the Section 287(g) program would radically weaken immigration law enforcement in the United States at a time when 12.5 million Americans are unemployed and competing with illegal foreign labor to find a job."[15] The 287(g) programs are vital to fighting problems associated with the war on terrorism and the problem of violent street gangs. Representative Steve King of Iowa pointed out in a congressional hearing that four of the 9/11 hijacker-terrorists in the United States illegally had been stopped by state and local law enforcement during their stay in the country. "All four were pulled over for traffic infractions at one point in the months before September 11, 2001," King said. "Unfortunately, none were reported to Federal immigration officials, despite their violations of Federal immigration laws. We all know the devastating results of the hijackers' malicious activities, and can only speculate how many lives might have been saved."[16] The reality is that, if local law enforcement had the power and resources to check and enforce the immigration status of those four terrorists, the 9/11 terrorist attacks may have been prevented.

Another pressing problem is that certain parts of the country are overrun by violent street gangs, such as the notorious Mara Salvatrucha-13 (MS-13) gang in Los Angeles. While MS-13 has spread to Central and South America, Los Angeles remains one of its primary bases of operation. Many—if not most—of the members of the MS-13 gang in Los Angeles and other cities are illegal immigrants. Professor Kobach explains that "Section 287(g) authority can be particularly useful in dealing with alien street gangs" and that "Section 287(g) authority enables those jurisdictions to continuously and routinely remove those illegally present gang members from the streets of our community."[17]

Criminal aliens account for nearly 30 percent of inmates in federal prisons, according to the Federal Bureau of Prisons.[18] Representative Lamar Smith of Texas said it best: "Those who are serious about public safety should not only support the [287(g)] program but also call for its expansion. We should do more, not less, to protect the lives and well-being of all Americans. We should do more to make our communities safer."[19]

Summary

Illegal immigration is a serious problem in the United States. Far too many people cross the U.S.-Mexico border illegally. Some of these individuals commit crimes and otherwise drain the resources of the United States. The U.S. Supreme Court and lower federal courts have consistently held that U.S. Border Patrol agents may consider race as one factor among many in their searches. Border Patrol agents should not be hamstrung from doing their tough jobs due to oversensitivity and political correctness.

Furthermore, the enforcement of federal immigration laws needs the assistance of local law enforcement officials who

QUOTABLE

Professor Kris W. Kobach

Section 287(g) is a program that has dramatically improved the rule of law in the immigration arena. It has provided vital support to an agency that has been chronically undermanned for decades. The Department of Justice originally, and the Department of Homeland Security now, have recognized the extraordinary value of this program. The departments have also recognized that one-size-fits-all is the wrong approach. Each 287(g) MOA is different, so that it meets the particular law enforcement needs of the jurisdiction in question. For Congress to attempt to put this program in a straightjacket would undercut the very flexibility that makes it so useful. For Congress to scale the program back or limit its scope would send a clear message that rigorous enforcement of our nation's immigration laws is not a congressional priority. Even worse, to do so at this time of economic crisis would be a grave disservice to the millions of unemployed U.S. citizens who are struggling to put food on the table, but finding that competition with unauthorized alien labor prevents them from doing so.

Source: Testimony of Kris W. Kobach at a hearing on "Public Safety and Civil Rights Implications of State and Local Enforcement of Federal Immigration Laws," before the House Committee on the Judiciary Subcommittee on Constitution, Civil Rights and Civil Liberties, April 2, 2009, http://judiciary.house.gov/hearings/pdf/Kobach090402.pdf.

often come into frequent contact with illegal immigrants. ICE agreements are a valuable law enforcement tool that should be respected and expanded. The safety of our country depends upon competent enforcement of illegal immigration. Although racial profiling has a bad name in the media, we must lose all perspective of racial realities. Some races simply have a large number of illegal immigrants. That is not profiling; that is a fact.

Profiling Latinos as Illegal Aliens Is Unconstitutional

In February 2009, 19-year-old Julio Cesar Mora of Avondale, Arizona, was riding with his father to their landscaping business in Phoenix. Two SUVs cut them off while they were driving. The SUVs contained officers with the Maricopa County Sheriff's Office. The officers forced Mora, a U.S. citizen, and his father, a legal resident, out of the car, searched them, and tied their hands together. The officers brought them to the landscaping business where the Moras worked, where about 80 other people were lined up along with numerous police officers, some of whom wore masks.

Mora's father asked to use the bathroom but was denied his request. An officer finally relented and allowed Mora's father to relieve himself near a police car. Later, three officers accompanied the younger Mora to the bathroom, but they refused to untie his hands. Mora and his father showed their Social Security cards, and the officers eventually let the pair go after three hours.

Mora felt extreme humiliation and embarrassment over the abject profiling:

> To this day, I don't know why the officers stopped us out of all the cars on the road. I don't think it is fair, the way we were treated. The police are supposed to keep us safe, but they are arresting us instead of the real criminals. I still think of that day sometimes, when I had to go to the bathroom in front of the police who mocked me. They took away our pride, my dad's and mine.[1]

Antonio Ramirez offered similar testimony to Congress about his plight as a Latino man in Frederick County, Maryland. He came to the United States from Mexico more than 20 years ago, initially working as a dishwasher at a restaurant. He became a naturalized citizen of the United States and now is the chief safety officer for a construction company. Though he loves America, he hates the racial profiling that he and his fellow Latinos have to endure. "In Frederick, Latinos are not seen as people anymore," he said. "Instead we are just 'illegals'— including many, like me, who are proud citizens of this great country."[2] Ramirez serves as a community leader for Latinos in Frederick County. He reported many recent instances of racial profiling to Congress. He told of the Latino man who was pulled over at 7:30 in the morning because a police officer said that the little air freshener tree hanging from his rearview mirror was blocking his view of the road. Two other Latino men were pulled over and ticketed by the police for driving too slowly. "Other Latinos—both immigrants and citizens—have said they have been stopped by police and asked for identification while they were just walking on the sidewalk or sitting on a bench. Most of them are also asked if they have drugs on them, and the police usually pat them down."[3]

Unfortunately, the plights of Julio Cesar Mora and Antonio Ramirez reflect a racial reality for many Latinos living in the

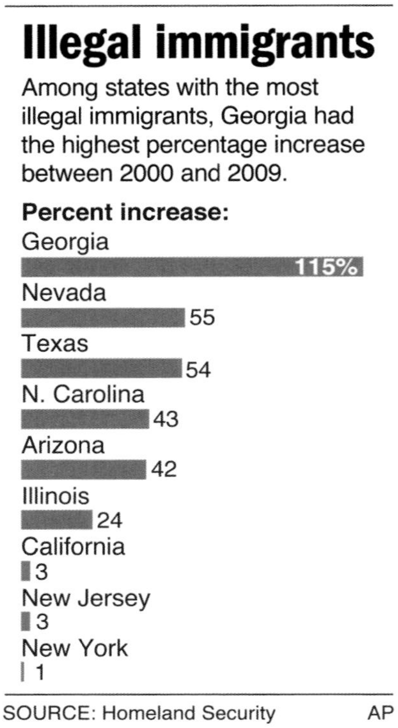

Illegal immigrants

Among states with the most
illegal immigrants, Georgia had
the highest percentage increase
between 2000 and 2009.

Percent increase:

Georgia
115%

Nevada
55

Texas
54

N. Carolina
43

Arizona
42

Illinois
24

California
3

New Jersey
3

New York
1

SOURCE: Homeland Security   AP

This chart shows the states with the highest percentage
increase of illegal immigrants in the last decade. In states
unused to large influxes of immigrants, people are often
stopped by police because of their race or ethnicity,
regardless of their status as citizens or legal immigrants.

United States. They are profiled based on their race or ethnicity, whether they are American citizens or not. Even federal
judges of Latino ancestry are not immune to racial profiling:
A border agent in Texas mistakenly assumed that federal judge
Filemon Vela was an illegal immigrant or drug smuggler.[4]

Latinos across the country worry that the nation's obsession with illegal immigration will harm them or a member of their family. A 2007 survey by the Pew Hispanic Center found that more than half of all Hispanic adults fear that a close friend or relative could be deported.[5]

Generally, race is not an acceptable factor for law enforcement to use.

The U.S. Supreme Court has made clear that law enforcement officials, including Border Patrol agents, need more than ethnic appearance in order to stop vehicles in a roving search. In *United States v. Brignoni-Ponce* (1975), Border Patrol agents admittedly stopped a car on a roving patrol solely because its occupants appeared to be of Mexican ancestry. The U.S. Supreme Court ruled that relying on race exclusively meant that the border

FROM THE BENCH

United States v. Brignoni-Ponce, 422 U.S. 873, 885-887 (1975)

In this case the officers relied on a single factor to justify stopping respondent's car: the apparent Mexican ancestry of the occupants. We cannot conclude that this furnished reasonable grounds to believe that the three occupants were aliens. At best the officers had only a fleeting glimpse of the persons in the moving car, illuminated by headlights. Even if they saw enough to think that the occupants were of Mexican descent, this factor alone would justify neither a reasonable belief that they were aliens, nor a reasonable belief that the car concealed other aliens who were illegally in the country. Large numbers of native-born and naturalized citizens have the physical characteristics identified with Mexican ancestry, and even in the border area a relatively small proportion of them are aliens. The likelihood that any given person of Mexican ancestry is an alien is high enough to make Mexican appearance a relative factor, but standing alone it does not justify stopping all Mexican-Americans to ask if they are aliens.

officers did not have reasonable suspicion to search the vehicle in question.[6]

Other courts have reiterated the view that the use of race alone as the sole or predominant factor in stopping vehicles is impermissible. In *United States v. Montero-Camargo* (2000),

---

FROM THE BENCH

United States v. Montero-Camargo, 208 F.3d 1122, 1132-1136 (9th Cir. 2000)

Brignoni-Ponce was handed down in 1975, some twenty-five years ago. Current demographic data demonstrate that the statistical premises on which its dictum relies are no longer applicable. The Hispanic population of this nation, and of the Southwest and Far West in particular, has grown enormously—at least five-fold in the four states referred to in the Supreme Court's decision. According to the U.S. Census Bureau, as of January 1, 2000, that population group stands at nearly 34 million. Furthermore, Hispanics are heavily concentrated in certain states in which minorities are becoming if not the majority, then at least the single largest group, either in the state as a whole or in a significant number of counties. According to the same data, California has the largest Hispanic population of any state—esti-mated at 10,112,986 in 1998, while Texas has approximately 6 million. As of this year, minorities—Hispanics, Asians, blacks and Native Americans—comprise half of California's residents; by 2021, Hispanics are expected to be the Golden State's largest group, making up about 40% of the state's population. Today, in Los Angeles County, which is by far the state's biggest population center, Hispanics already constitute the largest single group.

One area where Hispanics are heavily in the majority is El Centro, the site of the vehicle stop. As Agent Johnson acknowledged, the majority of the people who pass through the El Centro checkpoint are Hispanic. His testimony is in turn corroborated by more general demographic data from that area. The popula-tion of Imperial County, in which El Centro is located, is 73% Hispanic. In Impe-rial County, as of 1998, Hispanics accounted for 105,355 of the total population of 144,051. More broadly, according to census data, five Southern California counties are home to more than a fifth of the nation's Hispanic population. . . . During the current decade, Hispanics will become the single largest population group in Southern California, . . . and by 2040, will make up 59% of Southern for example, the U.S. Court of Appeals for the Ninth Circuit explained: "The likelihood that in an area in which the majority—or even a substantial part—of the population is Hispanic, any given person of Hispanic ancestry is in fact an alien, let alone an illegal alien, is not high enough to make Hispanic appearance

California's population. Accordingly, Hispanic appearance is of little or no use in determining which particular individuals among the vast Hispanic populace should be stopped by law enforcement officials on the lookout for illegal aliens. Reasonable suspicion requires *particularized* suspicion, and in an area in which a large number of people share a specific characteristic, that characteristic casts too wide a net to play any part in a particularized reasonable suspicion determination.

Moreover, the demographic changes we describe have been accompanied by significant changes in the law restricting the use of race as a criterion in government decision-making. The use of race and ethnicity for such purposes has been severely limited. . . . The danger of stigmatic harm of the type that the Court feared overbroad affirmative action programs would pose is far more pronounced in the context of police stops in which race or ethnic appearance is a factor. So, too, are the consequences of "notions of racial inferiority" and the "politics of racial hostility" that the Court pointed to. Stops based on race or ethnic appearance send the underlying message to all our citizens that those who are not white are judged by the color of their skin alone. Such stops also send a clear message that those who are not white enjoy a lesser degree of constitutional protection—that they are in effect assumed to be potential criminals first and individuals second. It would be an anomalous result to hold that race may be considered when it harms people, but not when it helps them. . . .

We decide no broad constitutional questions here. Rather, we are confronted with the narrow question of how to square the Fourth Amendment's requirement of individualized reasonable suspicion with the fact that the majority of the people who pass through the checkpoint in question are Hispanic. In order to answer that question, . . . we conclude that, at this point in our nation's history, and given the continuing changes in our ethnic and racial composition, Hispanic appearance is, in general, of such little probative value that it may not be considered as a relevant factor where particularized or individualized suspicion is required.

a relevant factor in the reasonable suspicion calculus."[7] In fact, the Ninth Circuit questioned whether the use of race could ever be a factor, particularly when the Hispanic population had grown so much since the mid-1970s when the Supreme Court decided *Brignoni-Ponce.* In many counties in Southern California, a sizable amount of the population is Hispanic. The population of one county in the area was 73 percent Hispanic. Because of the large number of Hispanics, it is not possible to say that race is a factor in determining whether a person is committing criminal activity, such as being in the country illegally. Such a policy would put far too many innocent people under the specter of suspicion. "Accordingly, Hispanic appearance is of little or no use in determining which particular individuals among the vast Hispanic populace should be stopped by law enforcement officials on the lookout for illegal aliens," wrote Judge Stephen Reinhardt for the Ninth Circuit. "Reasonable suspicion requires *particularized* suspicion, and in an area in which a large number of people share a specific characteristic, that characteristic casts too wide a net to play any part in a particularized reasonable suspicion determination."[8]

Current ICE agreements with local law enforcement have led to racial profiling.

The federal Immigration and Customs Enforcement (ICE) agency has instituted numerous policies to enforce federal immigration laws, including the establishment of the Border Enforcement Security Task Forces and the Criminal Alien Program. The most problematic of these programs is the Delegation of Immigration Authority program. Under this program, ICE enters into a Memorandum of Agreement (MOA) with state and local officials regarding the nation's immigration laws. The ICE agreements allow state and local government officials to function as the enforcers of federal immigration law. The American Civil Liberties Union (ACLU) warns that the result is that state and local government officials often "improperly rely on race or ethnicity as a proxy for undocumented status."[9] In other words, state and local government officials racially profile Latinos who they think are illegal immigrants.

Immigration raids frequently are nothing more than blatant racial profiling. "We're living in a state of fear," one Latino immigrant said. "We're not criminals. We're just here to work to feed our families."[10] Many border agents apparently only question Latinos and not any other race or ethnicity. Accusations of racial profiling continue to dog many Border Patrol agents when they raid work sites.[11] The problem is exacerbated due

---

QUOTABLE

Wade Henderson, president & CEO, Leadership Conference on Civil Rights

Local law enforcement of civil immigration laws under 287(g) agreements is a civil and human rights issue, not just an immigration issue. Although the program is promoted as one that allows local and state police to identify serious criminals who are noncitizens and facilitate their deportation once their sentence is completed, the reality of that program has been rampant racial profiling that has affected undocumented immigrants, legal residents and citizens....

Police officers have interpreted the authority from ICE to allow them to raid day laborer sites and use traffic stops to check people's immigration status. Citizens have been detained after traffic stops based on their name and accent, or even for listening to Spanish music while standing outside of a family business. Painting the program with a veneer of immigration enforcement does not accurately relay the nature of the program, nor does it cure the underlying violations....

The 287(g) program is part of a dangerous trend that can inhibit effective law enforcement and ultimately can endanger the lives of all persons who depend on law enforcement for protection. When local law enforcement begins targeting people for their suspected immigration status and not criminal activity, the entire community suffers.

Source: Testimony of Wade Henderson before the House Committee on the Judiciary, April 2, 2009.

to the ICE agreements; now local law enforcement officials, who have less training in immigration matters than border agents, engage in even starker racial profiling. The ACLU notes: "When local police function as immigration agents, the message is sent that some citizens do not deserve equal protection under the law."[12]

Summary

The profiling of Latinos in the United States is a pressing problem. In recent years, the anti-immigrant backlash and obsession over illegal aliens has often led to racial profiling. Such profiling violates the U.S. Supreme Court's warning that a person's race cannot be the sole factor for border agents or other law enforcement officials to stop and search anyone. Courts should go further, as the Ninth Circuit has done, and prohibit the use of appearance as a relevant factor. The ICE program that enables local law enforcement officials to serve as immigration agents has been particularly disastrous. Work raids turn into nothing more than abject racial profiling. Many Latinos live in fear of the harassment by law enforcement officials.

The Future of Racial Profiling

R acial profiling is a pervasive and controversial issue that continues to inspire debate and dialogue. People fundamentally disagree over what exactly constitutes racial profiling; whether race should play a role in the decision-making processes of law enforcement officers; whether societal concerns should trump concerns over individual rights of equality; and about how much larger issues, such as defending the border or prosecuting the war on terror, should play in determining whether profiling practices are constitutional.

Despite these debates, no one can dispute the fact that concerns about racial profiling have led to increased oversight by the executive and legislative branches of the U.S. government. The Department of Justice, for example, has weighed in on the issue of racial profiling numerous times through the years. In June 2003, the department issued a document entitled "Guidance Regarding the Use of Race by Federal Law Enforcement Agencies."[1] It explained the department's stance against racial profiling and provided examples—some of which were discussed previously—of what constitutes impermissible racial profiling. Presidents George W. Bush and Barack Obama have condemned the practice of racial profiling. In February 2001, President Bush declared: "It's wrong and we will end it in America."[2] President Obama, when asked about the Henry Louis Gates imbroglio, responded in part that "what I think we know separate and apart from this incident is that there's a long history in this country of African Americans and Latinos being stopped by law enforcement disproportionately. That's just a fact."[3]

Legislative Attempts to Address Racial Profiling

Many state legislatures have addressed the problem of racial profiling in a variety of ways. Some state laws bluntly say that no law enforcement officer shall engage in racial profiling. Other state laws require law enforcement agencies to adopt policies on racial profiling, to require training of officers to ensure against racial profiling, and to compile a database of racial profiling complaints.[4]

Some state laws, such as Kansas's law, even require law enforcement agencies to adopt policies for disciplining officers who engaged in racial profiling.[5] Other states require law enforcement agencies to work with minority communities to address the problem of racial profiling. Washington's law requires law enforcement agencies to "work with the minority groups in their community to appropriately address the issue of racial profiling."[6] California law requires that all law enforcement officers undergo "racial and cultural diversity training."[7]

In April 2010, Governor Jan Brewer of Arizona signed a state law designed to address legal immigration. Critics charge that the Arizona statute sanctions racial profiling.[8] As more information comes in through various data collection laws, government leaders and others will be able to see whether racial disparities continue

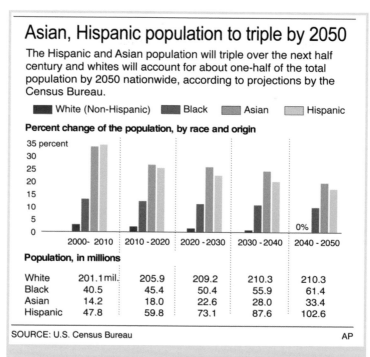

Asian, Hispanic population to triple by 2050

The Hispanic and Asian population will triple over the next half century and whites will account for about one-half of the total population by 2050 nationwide, according to projections by the Census Bureau.

■ White (Non-Hispanic)   ■ Black   ■ Asian   ▨ Hispanic

Percent change of the population, by race and origin

	2000-2010	2010-2020	2020-2030	2030-2040	2040-2050

Population, in millions

	2000-2010	2010-2020	2020-2030	2030-2040	2040-2050
White	201.1 mil.	205.9	209.2	210.3	210.3
Black	40.5	45.4	50.4	55.9	61.4
Asian	14.2	18.0	22.6	28.0	33.4
Hispanic	47.8	59.8	73.1	87.6	102.6

SOURCE: U.S. Census Bureau   AP

The above graphic projects the increase in Hispanic and Asian populations in the United States by 2050, if current immigration trends and birthrates hold firm. Such a change in demographics will likely impact the debate over racial profiling.

to exist with respect to traffic stops and other encounters with law enforcement officials.[9] The question at that time will then be whether the federal government will do more in the area of racial profiling. Measures have been introduced in the U.S. Congress to address racial profiling in the areas of the war on drugs[10] and border searches,[11] as well as to eliminate racial profiling in general. Perhaps the most ambitious proposal is the End Racial Profiling Act, which has been introduced in the 107th, 108th, 109th, and 110th sessions of Congress.

Representative John Conyers and Senator Russ Feingold are planning to introduce the measure again in 2010 in the 111th session of Congress. The measure would prohibit racial profiling by federal government officials and would require training in racial

---

THE LETTER OF THE LAW

Kansas Code of Criminal Procedure

Article 46: General Provisions

22-4610. Same; policies preempting profiling, requirements; annual reports of complaints.

(a) All law enforcement agencies in this state shall adopt a detailed, written policy to preempt racial profiling. Each agency's policy shall include the definition of racial profiling found in K.S.A. 22-4006, and amendments thereto.

(b) Policies adopted pursuant to this section shall be implemented by all Kansas law enforcement agencies within one year after the effective date of this act. The policies and data collection procedures shall be available for public inspection during normal business hours.

(c) The policies adopted pursuant to this section shall include, but not be limited to, the following:

(1) A prohibition of racial profiling.

(2) Annual educational training which shall include, but not be limited to, an understanding of the historical and cultural systems that perpetuate racial profiling, assistance in identifying racial profiling practices, and providing officers with self-evaluation strategies to preempt racial profiling prior to stopping a citizen.

(3) For law enforcement agencies of cities of the first class, establishment or use of current independent citizen advisory boards which include participants who reflect the racial and ethnic community, to advise and assist in policy development, education, and community outreach and communications related to racial profiling by law enforcement officers and agencies.

(4) Policies for discipline of law enforcement officers and agencies who engage in racial profiling.

profiling by federal law enforcement officials. Additionally, the proposed law would require the accumulation of data with respect to traffic stops and searches to determine whether the practice of

(continues on page 80)

(5) A provision that, if the investigation of a complaint of racial profiling reveals the officer was in direct violation of the law enforcement agency's written policies regarding racial profiling, the employing law enforcement agency shall take appropriate action consistent with applicable laws, rules and regulations, resolutions, ordinances or policies, including demerits, suspension or removal of the officer from the agency.

(6) Provisions for community outreach and communications efforts to inform the public of the individual's right to file with the law enforcement agency or the Kansas human rights commission complaints regarding racial profiling, which outreach and communications to the community shall include ongoing efforts to notify the public of the law enforcement agency's complaint process.

(7) Procedures for individuals to file complaints of racial profiling with the agency, which, if appropriate, may provide for use of current procedures for addressing such complaints.

(d) Each law enforcement agency shall compile an annual report of all complaints of racial profiling received and shall submit the report on or before January 31 to the office of the attorney general for review. The annual report shall include: (1) The date the complaint is filed; (2) action taken in response to the complaint; (3) the decision upon disposition of the complaint; and (4) the date the complaint is closed. Annual reports filed pursuant to this subsection shall be open public records and shall be posted on the official website of the attorney general.

Source: K.S.A. § 22-4610, http://kansasstatutes.lesterama.org/Chapter_22/Article_46/#22-4610.html.

Federal Legislative Proposal: Excerpts from the End Racial Profiling Act of 2007

(a) Findings- Congress finds the following:

(1) Federal, State, and local law enforcement agents play a vital role in protecting the public from crime and protecting the Nation from terrorism. The vast majority of law enforcement agents nationwide discharge their duties professionally and without bias.

(2) The use by police officers of race, ethnicity, national origin, or religion in deciding which persons should be subject to traffic stops, stops and frisks, questioning, searches, and seizures is improper.

(3) In his address to a joint session of Congress on February 27, 2001, President George W. Bush declared that "racial profiling is wrong and we will end it in America." He directed the Attorney General to implement this policy.

(4) In June 2003, the Department of Justice issued a Policy Guidance regarding racial profiling by Federal law enforcement agencies which stated: "Racial profiling in law enforcement is not merely wrong, but also ineffective. Race-based assumptions in law enforcement perpetuate negative racial stereotypes that are harmful to our rich and diverse democracy, and materially impair our efforts to maintain a fair and just society."

(5) The Department of Justice Guidance is a useful first step, but does not achieve the President's stated goal of ending racial profiling in America, as—

(A) it does not apply to State and local law enforcement agencies;

(B) it does not contain a meaningful enforcement mechanism;

(C) it does not require data collection; and

(D) it contains an overbroad exception for immigration and national security matters.

(6) Current efforts by State and local governments to eradicate racial profiling and redress the harms it causes, while also laudable, have been limited in scope and insufficient to address this national problem. Therefore, Federal legislation is needed.

(7) Statistical evidence from across the country demonstrates that racial profiling is a real and measurable phenomenon.

(8) As of November 15, 2000, the Department of Justice had 14 publicly noticed, ongoing, pattern or practice investigations involving allegations of racial profiling and had filed 5 pattern or practice lawsuits involving allegations of racial profiling, with 4 of those cases resolved through consent decrees.

(9) A large majority of individuals subjected to stops and other enforcement activities based on race, ethnicity, national origin, or religion are found to be law abiding and therefore racial profiling is not an effective means to uncover criminal activity.

(10) A 2001 Department of Justice report on citizen-police contacts that occurred in 1999 found that, although Blacks and Hispanics were more likely to be stopped and searched, they were less likely to be in possession of contraband. On average, searches and seizures of Black drivers yielded evidence only 8 percent of the time, searches and seizures of Hispanic drivers yielded evidence only 10 percent of the time, and searches and seizures of White drivers yielded evidence 17 percent of the time. . . .

(12) A 2005 report of the Bureau of Justice Statistics of the Department of Justice on citizen-police contacts that occurred in 2002, found that, although Whites, Blacks, and Hispanics were stopped by the police at the same rate—

(A) Blacks and Hispanics were much more likely to be arrested than Whites;

(B) Hispanics were much more likely to be ticketed than Blacks or Whites;

(C) Blacks and Hispanics were much more likely to report the use or threatened use of force by a police officer;

(D) Blacks and Hispanics were much more likely to be handcuffed than Whites; and

(E) Blacks and Hispanics were much more likely to have their vehicles searched than Whites. . . .

(14) Racial profiling harms individuals subjected to it because they experience fear, anxiety, humiliation, anger, resentment, and cynicism when they are unjustifiably treated as criminal suspects. By discouraging individuals from traveling freely, racial profiling impairs both interstate and intrastate commerce.

(continues)

(continued)

(15) Racial profiling damages law enforcement and the criminal justice system as a whole by undermining public confidence and trust in the police, the courts, and the criminal law. . . .

(19) A comprehensive national solution is needed to address racial profiling at the Federal, State, and local levels. Federal support is needed to combat racial profiling through specialized training of law enforcement agents, improved management systems, and the acquisition of technology such as in-car video cameras.

Source: http://www.govtrack.us/congress/billtext.xpd?bill=h110-4611.

(continued from page 77)

racial profiling continues and to what extent. The measure already has the full support of the American Bar Association (ABA).[12]

Summary

Debate on racial profiling will not end anytime soon, particularly when law enforcement must prosecute drug laws, provide national security, and enforce the nation's immigration laws while still protecting individuals' constitutional freedoms to equal protection of the laws and freedom from unreasonable searches and seizures. There is no doubt that the nation faces grave national security threats. To combat these threats, the Department of Homeland Security has stepped up its use of technology that assists it in behavioral profiling. "Rather than investigate particular plots or actual, known suspects, the United States and other governments are developing new tools to make quick evaluations of whether individuals might be dangerous," commentators Justin Florence and Robert Friedman write. "Rather than rely on explicit racial or religious profiling, they purport to use objective, scientific criteria to identify dangerous people by analyzing their facial movements, voices, blood pressure, sweat levels, heart and breathing rates, and even brain waves."[13] Perhaps this new form of profiling will eventually supersede the use of race or religion in criminal profiling. For the foreseeable future, however, the debate over racial profiling—as the dispute in Arizona shows—will continue as the nation calibrates the balance between the competing concerns of individual liberty and national security.

Beginning Legal Research

The goals of each book in the POINT/COUNTERPOINT series are not only to give the reader a basic introduction to a controversial issue affecting society, but also to encourage the reader to explore the issue more fully. This Appendix is meant to serve as a guide to the reader in researching the current state of the law as well as exploring some of the public policy arguments as to why existing laws should be changed or new laws are needed.

Although some sources of law can be found primarily in law libraries, legal research has become much faster and more accessible with the advent of the Internet. This Appendix discusses some of the best starting points for free access to laws and court decisions, but surfing the Web will uncover endless additional sources of information. Before you can research the law, however, you must have a basic understanding of the American legal system.

The most important source of law in the United States is the Constitution. Originally enacted in 1787, the Constitution outlines the structure of our federal government, as well as setting limits on the types of laws that the federal government and state governments can enact. Through the centuries, a number of amendments have added to or changed the Constitution, most notably the first 10 amendments, which collectively are known as the "Bill of Rights" and which guarantee important civil liberties.

Reading the plain text of the Constitution provides little information. For example, the Constitution prohibits "unreasonable searches and seizures" by the police. To understand concepts in the Constitution, it is necessary to look to the decisions of the U.S. Supreme Court, which has the ultimate authority in interpreting the meaning of the Constitution. For example, the U.S. Supreme Court's 2001 decision in *Kyllo v. United States* held that scanning the outside of a person's house using a heat sensor to determine whether the person is growing marijuana is an unreasonable search—if it is done without first getting a search warrant from a judge. Each state also has its own constitution and a supreme court that is the ultimate authority on its meaning.

Also important are the written laws, or "statutes," passed by the U.S. Congress and the individual state legislatures. As with constitutional provisions, the U.S. Supreme Court and the state supreme courts are the ultimate authorities in interpreting the meaning of federal and state laws, respectively. However, the U.S. Supreme Court might find that a state law violates the U.S. Constitution, and a state supreme court might find that a state law violates either the state or U.S. Constitution.

Not every controversy reaches either the U.S. Supreme Court or the state supreme courts, however. Therefore, the decisions of other courts are also important. Trial courts hear evidence from both sides and make a decision, while appeals courts review the decisions made by trial courts. Sometimes rulings from appeals courts are appealed further to the U.S. Supreme Court or the state supreme courts.

Lawyers and courts refer to statutes and court decisions through a formal system of citations. Use of these citations reveals which court made the decision or which legislature passed the statute, and allows one to quickly locate the statute or court case online or in a law library. For example, the Supreme Court case *Brown v. Board of Education* has the legal citation 347 U.S. 483 (1954). At a law library, this 1954 decision can be found on page 483 of volume 347 of the U.S. Reports, which are the official collection of the Supreme Court's decisions. On the following page, you will find samples of all the major kinds of legal citation.

Finding sources of legal information on the Internet is relatively simple thanks to "portal" sites such as findlaw.com and lexisone.com, which allow the user to access a variety of constitutions, statutes, court opinions, law review articles, news articles, and other useful sources of information. For example, findlaw.com offers access to all Supreme Court decisions since 1893. Other useful sources of information include gpo.gov, which contains a complete copy of the U.S. Code, and thomas.loc.gov, which offers access to bills pending before Congress, as well as recently passed laws. Of course, the Internet changes every second of every day, so it is best to do some independent searching.

Of course, many people still do their research at law libraries, some of which are open to the public. For example, some state governments and universities offer the public access to their law collections. Law librarians can be of great assistance, as even experienced attorneys need help with legal research from time to time.

Common Citation Forms

Source of Law	Sample Citation	Notes
U.S. Supreme Court	*Employment Division v. Smith*, 485 U.S. 660 (1988)	The U.S. Reports is the official record of Supreme Court decisions. There is also an unofficial Supreme Court ("S. Ct.") reporter.
U.S. Court of Appeals	*United States v. Lambert*, 695 F.2d 536 (11th Cir.1983)	Appellate cases appear in the Federal Reporter, designated by "F." The 11th Circuit has jurisdiction in Alabama, Florida, and Georgia.
U.S. District Court	*Carillon Importers, Ltd. v. Frank Pesce Group, Inc.*, 913 F.Supp. 1559 (S.D.Fla.1996)	Federal trial-level decisions are reported in the Federal Supplement ("F. Supp."). Some states have multiple federal districts; this case originated in the Southern District of Florida.
U.S. Code	Thomas Jefferson Commemoration Commission Act, 36 U.S.C., §149 (2002)	Sometimes the popular names of legislation—names with which the public may be familiar—are included with the U.S. Code citation.
State Supreme Court	*Sterling v. Cupp*, 290 Ore. 611, 614, 625 P.2d 123, 126 (1981)	The Oregon Supreme Court decision is reported in both the state's reporter and the Pacific regional reporter.
State Statute	Pennsylvania Abortion Control Act of 1982, 18 Pa. Cons. Stat. 3203-3220 (1990)	States use many different citation formats for their statutes.

Cases

United States v. Brignoni-Ponce, 422 U.S. 873 (1975)

In this decision, the U.S. Supreme Court reversed a lower court finding that a roving Border Patrol search of Hispanic men was constitutional under the Fourth Amendment. The Court, however, also determined that race or ethnicity could be a permissible factor in the determination as to whether the Border Patrol agents had the proper reasonable suspicion.

United States v. Mendenhall, 446 U.S. 544 (1980)

In this decision, the U.S. Supreme Court ruled that DEA officials did not violate the Fourth Amendment rights of a woman suspected of fitting a drug courier profile in an airport. The Court ruled that the woman gave consent to the subsequent search that found drugs. The Court did rule that individuals' Fourth Amendment rights could be violated if they are surrounded by agents and do not feel free to leave.

United States v. Berry, 670 F.2d 583 (5th Cir. 1982)

In this lower court decision, a federal appeals court identified the primary and secondary characteristics of the drug courier profile as compiled by experienced DEA agents.

United States v. Sokolow, 490 U.S. 1 (1989)

In this decision, the U.S. Supreme Court ruled that officers had enough suspicion to search an airline passenger who, as it turned out, was carrying large amounts of narcotics. The Court determined that the use of the drug courier profile did not invalidate the search because factors in the compilation of the profile might have some evidentiary significance.

State v. Williams, 525 N.W.2d 538 (Minn. 1994)

In this decision, the Minnesota Supreme Court rejected the use of the drug courier profile and ruled that a defendant's Fourth Amendment rights had been violated by its usage. The court warned that the profile could camouflage racial discrimination.

United States v. Montero-Camargo, 208 F.3d 1122 (9th Cir. 2000)

In this decision, the U.S. Court of Appeals for the Ninth Circuit determined that race or ethnicity could not be used as a relevant factor in a law enforcement official's determination of whether there was reasonable suspicion that someone was an illegal immigrant.

United States v. Bautista-Silva, 567 F.3d 1266 (11th Cir. 2009)

In this decision, the U.S. Court of Appeals for the Eleventh Circuit ruled that race or ethnicity could be one of many factors in determining whether a Border Patrol agent had reasonable suspicion to stop a vehicle containing Hispanic men.

Terms and Concepts

Border Patrol agents

Criminal profiling

Department of Justice

Drug courier profile

Drug Enforcement Administration (DEA)

Equal Protection Clause

Fourteenth Amendment

Fourth Amendment

Immigration

Immigration and Customs Enforcement (ICE)

Probable cause

Racial profiling

Reasonable suspicion

Introduction: An Overview of Racial Profiling

1 Krissah Thompson, "Scholar Says Arrest Will Lead Him to Explore Race in Criminal Justice," *Washington Post*, July 22, 2009, http://www.washingtonpost.com/wp-dyn/content/article/2009/07/21/AR2009072101771.html.

2 Krissah Thompson and Cheryl W. Thompson, "Officer Tells His Side of the Story in Gates Arrest," *Washington Post*, July 24, 2009, http://www.washingtonpost.com/wp-dyn/content/article/2009/07/23/AR2009072301073.html?sid=ST2009072301777.

3 Michael A. Fletcher and Michael D. Shear, "Obama Voices Regret to Policeman," *Washington Post*, July 25, 2009, http://www.washingtonpost.com/wp-dyn/content/story/2009/07/23/ST2009072301777.html?sid=ST2009072301777.

4 David McLemore, "Drug Raid Changed Landscape; 1999 Sting Brought Attention, Racial Strife to Panhandle Town," *Dallas Morning News*, June 15, 2003, p. 10A.

5 Nate Blakeslee, *Tulia: Race, Cocaine, and Corruption in a Small Texas Town*. New York: Public Affairs, 2005.

6 Benjamin Todd Jealous and Margaret Huang, "End Racial Profiling Now," *Baltimore Sun*, December 7, 2009, p. 13A.

7 Department of Justice, "Fact Sheet: Racial Profiling," June 17, 2003, http://www.justice.gov/opa/pr/2003/June/racial_profiling_fact_sheet.pdf.

8 Heather MacDonald, "Racial Profiling Does Not Exist," in *Racial Profiling*. Florence, Ky.: Cengage Learning, 2009, p. 37.

9 Amnesty International, "Threat and Humiliation: Racial Profiling, Domestic Security, and Human Rights in the United States," September 2004, p. v. http://www.amnestyusa.org/racial_profiling/report/rp_report.pdf.

10 Rev. Code Wash. (ARCW) § 43.101.410.

11 Department of Justice, "Fact Sheet: Racial Profiling," June 17, 2003, http://www.justice.gov/opa/pr/2003/June/racial_profiling_fact_sheet.pdf.

12 Quoted in Alison Bath, "Q&A: Law Enforcement Expert Explains Criminal, Racial Profiling," *Times* (Shreveport, La.), January 20, 2008, p. 5A.

Point: The Drug Courier Profile Is Effective in Combating the War on Drugs

1 Quoted in Jodi Wilgoren, "Police Profiling Debate Hinges on Issue of Experience vs. Bias," *New York Times*, April 9, 1999, p. B1.

2 Milton Heumann and Lance Cassak, *Good Cop, Bad Cop: Racial Profiling and Competing Views of Justice*. New York: Peter Lang Publishing, 2003, p. 41.

3 *U.S. v. Berry*, 670 F.2d 583, 600 at n. 21 (5th Cir. 1982).

4 Quoted in David A. Harris, *Profiles in Injustice: Why Racial Profiling Cannot Work*. New York: The New Press, 2003, p. 21.

5 Jim Mann, "Drug Runner Profile: Is It a Fair Weapon?" *Los Angeles Times*, March 14, 1980, p. B1.

6 *U.S. v. Elmore*, 595 F.2d 1036, 1039 (5th Cir. 1982).

7 *U.S. v. Mendenhall*, 446 U.S. 544 (1980).

8 Ibid., at 548.

9 Ibid., at 543.

10 Ibid., at 565.

11 *U.S. v. Sokolow*, 490 U.S. 1 (1989).

12 Ibid. at 1–2.

13 *U.S. v. Mincey*, 321 Fed. Appx. 233, 242 (4th Cir. 2008).

14 Brian A. Wilson, "The War on Drugs: Evening the Odds through the Use of the Airport Drug Courier Profile," 6 *Boston University Public Interest Law Journal* 203, 205 (1996).

15 Mark W. Dunderdale, "Totality of the Suspicious Circumstances: Airport Drug Courier Profile Use in Massachusetts Since *Commonwealth v. Torres*," 5 *Suffolk Journal of Trial and Appellate Advocacy*. 125, 148 (2000).

Counterpoint: The Drug Courier Profile Leads to Racial Discrimination

1 Katheryn Russell-Brown, *The Color of Crime* (2nd ed.). New York: New York University Press, 2009, p. 72.

2 Henry Goldman and Thomas Ginsberg, "Use of Racial Profiling on Drivers

Meets More Legal Challenges," *Dallas Morning News*, March 7, 1999, p. 18A.

3 Quoted in Katheryn Russell-Brown, *The Color of Crime* (2nd ed.), p. 72.

4 Russell L. Jones, "A More Perfect Nation: Ending Racial Profiling," 41 *Valparaiso University Law Review* 621, 629 (2006).

5 David A. Harris, *Profiles in Injustice*, p. 63.

6 *U.S. v. Berry*, 670 F.2d 583, 599 (5th Cir. 1982).

7 Ibid.

8 *United States v. Hooper*, 935 F.2d 484, 499 (2nd Cir. 1991) (J. Pratt, dissenting).

9 Ibid.

10 *United States v. Weaver*, 966 F.2d 391, 397 (8th Cir. 1992) (J. Arnold, dissenting).

11 *United States v. Avery*, 137 F.3d 343, 354–356 (6th Cir. 1998).

12 *State v. Williams*, 525 N.W.2d 538, 547 (Minn. 1994).

13 Kevin R. Johnson, "Taking the 'Garbage' Out in Tulia, Texas: The Taboo on Black-White Romance and Racial Profiling in the 'War on Drugs,'" 2007 *Wisconsin Law Review* 283, 310 (2007).

14 David A. Harris, *Profiles in Injustice*, p. 79.

Point: Some Racial Profiling Is Necessary in the War on Terror

1 *9/11 Commission Report*, p. 1, http://govinfo.library.unt.edu/911/report/911Report_Ch1.pdf.

2 *9/11 Commission Report*, pp. 386–387, http://govinfo.library.unt.edu/911/report/911Report_Ch12.pdf.

3 Philip Sherwell and Alex Spillius, "Fort Hood Shooting: Texas Army Killer Linked to September 11th Terrorists," *Telegraph*, November 7, 2009, http://www.telegraph.co.uk/news/worldnews/northamerica/usa/6521758/Fort-Hood-shooting-Texas-army-killer-linked-to-September-11-terrorists.html.

4 Steven Emerson, "Screening Must Include Religion, Ethnicity," Investigative Project on Terrorism, January 5, 2010.

5 Newt Gingrich, "On Terrorism It's Time to Know, to Profile, and to Discriminate," HumanEvents.

com, December 30, 2009, http://www.humanevents.com/article.php?print=yes&id=35025.

6 Ibid.

7 Rod Dreher, "Will We Ever Wake Up to Islamic Radical Threat?" *Dallas Morning News*, November 13, 2009, http://www.dallasnews.com/sharedcontent/dws/dn/opinion/columnists/rdreher/stories/DN-dreher_1115edi.State.Edition1.20926f8.html.

8 See Williams's redacted memo at http://www.thesmokinggun.com/archive/0412042phoenix1.html.

9 Michelle Malkin, "Racial Profiling: A Matter of Survival," *USA Today*, August 17, 2004, p. 13A.

10 Paul Quinlan, "Profile Muslims, Flanagan Says; It Would Make Flying Safer," *Sarasota Herald-Tribune*, August 26, 2006, p. BS1.

11 Sharon R. Reddick, "Arab Muslims Should Be Profiled by the Government," in *Racial Profiling*. Farmington Hills, Mich.: Greenhaven Press, 2009, p. 89.

12 Scott Rasmussen, "Rasmussen Poll: 59% Favor Racial, Ethnic Profiling at Airports," January 7, 2010, http://www.rasmussenreports.com/public_content/lifestyle/general_lifestyle/january_2010/59_favor_racial_ethnic_profiling_for_airline_security.

13 Jeff P. Emanuel, "War on Terror; Profiling Also Fits into Puzzle," *Atlanta Journal-Constitution*, September 1, 2006, p. A11.

14 Rachel Ehrenfeld, "Should Profiling Be Used to Identify Potential Terrorists?" *Duluth News-Tribune*, August 22, 2005.

15 Kathleen Parker, "All Is Fair in War Except Insensitivity," *Sun Sentinel*, September 26, 2001, p. 19A.

Counterpoint: Racial Profiling in the War on Terror Is Wrong and Costly

1 Maudlyne Ihejirika, "Protestors Demand End to Arab-American 'Profiling,'" *Chicago Sun-Times*, February 22, 2004, p. 21.

2 Brian Skoloff, "FBI's Dragnet Frightens Muslims," Associated Press, September 26, 2001.

3   Amnesty International, "Threat and Humiliation: Racial Profiling, Domestic Security, and Human Rights in the United States," September 2004, pp. 1, 5, http://www.amnestyusa.org/racial_profiling/report/rp_report.pdf.

4   Riad Z. Abdelkarim, M.D., "Arab and Muslim Americans: Collateral Damage in the Wars on Terrorism, Iraq," Washington Report on Middle East Affairs, May 2003, http://www.wrmea.com/archives/may03/0305055.html.

5   Abdus Sattar Ghazali, "American Muslims Eight Years After 9/11," September 9, 2009, http://www.watan.com/en/the-community/636-abdus-sattar-ghazali.html.

6   Council on American-Islamic Relations, "Islamophobia," http://www.cair.com/Issues/Islamophobia/Islamophobia.aspx.

7   Rashad Hussain, "Preventing the New Internment: A Security-Sensitive Standard for Equal Protection Claims in the Post-9/11 Era," 13 Texas Journal on Civil Liberties & Civil Rights 117, 136 (2007).

8   Hussain, "Preventing the New Internment," p. 137.

9   American-Arab Anti-Discrimination Committee, "NSEERS: The Consequences of America's Efforts to Secure Its Borders. March 31, 2009, http://www.adc.org/PDF/nseerspaper.pdf.

10 Amnesty International, "Threat and Humiliation," p. 16.

11 Thomas Ginsberg, "Targeted Deportations Rise; the Number of Arabs and Muslims Ousted from the U.S. Nearly Doubled," Philadelphia Inquirer, June 18, 2003, p. A11.

12 Eric Lichtblau, "F.B.I. Tells Offices to Count Local Muslims and Mosques," New York Times, January 28, 2003, p. A13.

13 Deborah Ramirez and Stephanie Woldenberg, "Balancing Security and Liberty in a Post-September 11th World: The Search for Common Sense in Domestic Counterterrorism Policy," 14 Temple Political & Civil Rights Law Review 495, 496 (2005).

14 Amnesty International, "Threat and Humiliation," p. 24.

15 Harris, Profiles in Injustice, p. 230.

16 Deborah Ramirez and Stephanie Woldenberg, "Balancing Security and Liberty in a Post-September 11th World," 14 Temple Political & Civil Rights Law Review 495, 495 (2005).

17 Ibid.

18 Hussain, "Preventing the New Internment," p. 154.

19 Amnesty International, "Threat and Humiliation," p. 21.

20 Ibid., p. 22.

21 Hussain, "Preventing the New Internment," p. 155.

22 Ibid., pp. 155–156.

23 Moustafa Bayoumi, "One Year Later: Muslims Are Caricatured, Unjustly Treated," Tallahassee Democrat, September 8, 2002, p. E2.

24 Anti-Defamation League, "Terrorism Strikes America: ADL Responds to Violence and Harassment Against Arab Americans and Muslim Americans," http://www.adl.org/terrorism_america/adl_responds.asp.

25 Civilrights.org, "Hate Crimes Against Arab Americans, Muslims and Sikhs," in "Confronting the New Faces of Hate: Hate Crimes in America 2009," http://www.civilrights.org/publications/hate-crimes/arab-americans.html.

Point: Some Racial Profiling Is Necessary to Combat Illegal Immigration

1   Testimony of Ray Tranchant, Joint Hearing before the House Committee on Judiciary Subcommittee on Immigration, Citizenship, Refugees, Border Security, and International Law and the Subcommittee on the Constitution, Civil Rights, and Civil Liberties, "Public Safety and Civil Rights Implications of State and Local Enforcement of Federal Immigration Laws," April 2, 2009, http://judiciary.house.gov/hearings/pdf/Tranchant090402.pdf.

2   Ibid.

3   News Release, "Jones Introduces Illegal Alien Crime Reporting Act," January 13, 2009.

4   United States v. Brignoni-Ponce, 422 U.S. 873, 886–887 (1975).

5   Ibid., p. 881.

6 Ibid., p. 885.
7 *United States v. Aldo Antonio Hernandez-Moya*, 2009 U.S. App. LEXIS 25886, No. 08-51128 (5th Cir.) (November 25, 2009).
8 Ibid., p. 7.
9 *United States v. Bautista-Silva*, 567 F.3d 1266 (11th Cir. 2009).
10 Jeffrey S. Passel, "The Size and Characteristics of the Unauthorized Migrant Population in the U.S., Estimates Based on the March 2005 Current Population Survey," March 7, 2006, http://pewhispanic.org/files/reports/61.pdf.
11 "Racial Profiling or Racial Reality?" *Chattanooga Times Free Press*, October 1, 2007, p. B9.
12 "Terrorists Use Mexico to Enter the U.S., Says Minuteman Founder," *New York Beacon*, June 14, 2007, p. 6.
13 Jack Martin, "Backsliding on National Security: The Immigration Connection," http://www.fairus.org/site/DocServer/healthcare_09.pdf?docID=3501.
14 8 U.S.C. § 1357(g).
15 Testimony of Kris W. Kobach, "Public Safety and Civil Rights Implications of State and Local Enforcement of Federal Immigration Laws," before the House Committee on Judiciary Subcommittee on Constitution, Civil Rights and Civil Liberties and Subcommittee on Immigration, Citizenship, Refugee, Border Security, and International Law, April 2, 2009, p. 6, http://judiciary.house.gov/hearings/pdf/Kobach090402.pdf.
16 Statement of Rep. Steve King, Joint Hearing on "Public Safety and Civil Rights Implications of State and Local Enforcement of Federal Immigration Laws," No. 111–19, p. 4, http://judiciary.house.gov/hearings/printers/111th/111-19_48439.PDF.
17 Kobach, pp. 10–11.
18 Greg Ball, "287(g) Is Needed to Protect against Criminal Illegal Immigrants," *Journal News*, April 30, 2008, p. 6B.
19 Statement of Rep. Lamar Smith, Joint Hearing on "Public Safety and Civil Rights Implications of State and Local Enforcement of Federal Immigration Laws," p. 7, http://judiciary.house.gov/hearings/printers/111th/111-19_48439.PDF.

Counterpoint: Profiling Latinos as Illegal Aliens Is Unconstitutional

1 Testimony of Julio Cesar Mora at Joint Hearing on "Public Safety and Civil Rights Implications of State and Local Enforcement of Federal Immigration Laws," No. 111–19, April 2, 2009, pp. 9–10, http://judiciary.house.gov/hearings/printers/111th/111-19_48439.PDF.
2 Testimony of Antonio Ramirez, Joint Hearing on the "Public Safety and Civil Rights Implications of State and Local Enforcement of Federal Immigration Law," No. 111–19, April 2, 2009, http://judiciary.house.gov/hearings/pdf/Ramirez090402.pdf.
3 Ibid.
4 Jim Yardley, "Border Patrol Effective, But Often Stops Wrong People," *Pittsburgh Post-Gazette*, January 30, 2000, p. A-20.
5 Pew Hispanic Center, "2007 National Survey of Latinos: As Illegal Immigration Issue Heats Up, Hispanics Feel a Chill," December 19, 2007, p. 1, http://pewhispanic.org/files/reports/84.pdf.
6 *United States v. Brignoni-Ponce*, 422 U.S. 873, 886–887 (1975).
7 *United States v. Montero-Camargo*, 208 F.3d 1122, 1132 (9th Cir. 2000).
8 Ibid., at 1134.
9 American Civil Liberties Union, "The Persistence of Racial and Ethnic Profiling in the United States: A Followup Report to the U.N. Committee on the Elimination of Racial Discrimination," August 2009, pp. 24–25, http://www.aclu.org/files/pdfs/humanrights/cerd_finalreport.pdf.
10 Quoted in Stephen Wall, "Protesters Denounce Immigration Raids," *San Bernardino County Sun*, December 31, 2008.
11 David Olson, "Inland Latinos Say Border Patrol Engages in Racial Profiling," *The Press Enterprise*, March 2, 2009.
12 ACLU, "The Persistence of Racial and Ethnic Profiling in the United States," p. 26.

Conclusion: The Future of Racial Profiling

1 See U.S. Department of Justice, "Guidance Regarding the Use of Race by Federal Law Enforcement Agencies," June 2003, http://www.justice.gov/crt/split/documents/guidance_on_race.php.

2 Quoted in Department of Justice, "Fact Sheet: Racial Profiling," p. 1, http://www.justice.gov/opa/pr/2003/June/racial_profiling_fact_sheet.pdf (statement delivered by Bush in February 27, 2001).

3 News Conference of the President, July 22, 2009, http://www.whitehouse.gov/the_press_office/News-Conference-by-the-President-July-22-2009/.

4 See Racial Profiling Data Collection Resource Center, http://www.racialprofilinganalysis.neu.edu/legislation/.

5 K.S.A. § 22-4610.

6 Rev. Code Wash. (ARCW) § 43.101.410

7 Cal Pen Code § 13519.4

8 Randall C. Archibold, "Arizona Enacts Stringent Law on Immigration," *New York Times*, April 23, 2010, http://www.nytimes.com/2010/04/24/us/politics/24immig.html.

9 See "Background and Current Data Collection Efforts: Introduction to Data Collection," Racial Profiling Data Collection Resource Center, http://www.racialprofilinganalysis.neu.edu/background/index.php.

10 H.R. 68, No More Tulias: Drug Law Enforcement Evidentiary Standards Improvement Act of 2009, 111th Congress—1st Session.

11 H.R. 1726, Border Security Search Accountability Act of 2009, 111th Congress—1st Session.

12 Letter from the American Bar Association to Representative John Conyers to express support for End Racial Profiling bill, December 1, 2009, http://www.abanet.org/poladv/letters/crimlaw/2009dec01_ERPAh_l.pdf.

13 Justin Florence and Robert Friedman, "Profiles in Terror: A Legal Framework for the Behavioral Profiling Paradigm," 17 *George Mason Law Review* 423 (2010).

RESOURCES ▷

Books and Articles

American-Arab Anti-Discrimination Committee. "NSEERS: The Consequences of America's Efforts to Secure Its Borders, March 31, 2009. Available online. URL: http://www.adc.org/PDF/nseerspaper.pdf.

American Civil Liberties Union. "The Persistence of Racial and Ethnic Profiling in the United States: A Followup Report to the U.N. Committee on the Elimination of Racial Discrimination," August 2009. Available online. URL: http://www.aclu.org/files/pdfs/humanrights/cerd_finalreport.pdf.

Amnesty International. "Threat and Humiliation: Racial Profiling, Domestic Security, and Human Rights in the United States," September 2004. Available online. URL: http://www.amnestyusa.org/racial_profiling/report/rp_report.pdf.

Becton, Charles L. "The Drug Courier Profile: 'All Seems Infected that th' Infected Spy, as All Looks Yellow to the Jaundic'd Eye.'" 65 *North Carolina Law Review* 417 (1987).

Blakeslee, Nate. *Tulia: Race, Cocaine, and Corruption in a Small Texas Town.* New York: Public Affairs, 2005.

Cole, David. *No Equal Justice: Race and Class in the American Criminal Justice System.* New York: The New Press, 2000.

Crouch, Stanley. "Wake Up: Arabs Should Be Profiled." *St. Louis Post-Dispatch*, March 19, 2002, B7.

Davis, Angela J. "Race, Cops, and Traffic Stops." 51 *University of Miami Law Review* 425 (1997).

Department of Justice. "Fact Sheet: Racial Profiling," June 17, 2003. Available online. URL: http://www.justice.gov/opa/pr/2003/June/racial_profiling_fact_sheet.pdf.

Dunderdale, Mark W. "Totality of the Suspicious Circumstances: Airport Drug Courier Profile Use in Massachusetts Since *Commonwealth v. Torres.*" 5 *Suffolk Journal of Trial and Appellate Advocacy* 125 (2000).

Florence, Justin, and Robert Friedman. "Profiles in Terror: A Legal Framework for the Behavioral Profiling Paradigm." 17 *George Mason Law Review* 423 (2010).

Harris, David A. *Profiles in Injustice: Why Racial Profiling Cannot Work.* New York: The New Press, 2003.

———. "Racial Profiling Redux." 22 *St. Louis University Public Law Review* 73 (2003).

———. "The Stories, the Statistics, and the Law: Why 'Driving While Black' Matters." 84 *Minnesota Law Review* 265 (1999).

Heumann, Milton, and Lance Cassak. *Good Cop, Bad Cop: Racial Profiling and Competing Views of Justice.* New York: Peter Lang Publishing, 2003.

Hussain, Rashad. "Preventing the New Internment: A Security-Sensitive Standard for Equal Protection Claims in the Post-9/11 Era." 13 *Texas Journal on Civil Liberties & Civil Rights* 117 (2007).

Johnson, Kevin R. "Taking the 'Garbage' Out in Tulia, Texas: The Taboo on Black-White Romance and Racial Profiling in the 'War on Drugs.'" 2007 *Wisconsin Law Review* 283 (2007).

Jones, Russell L. "A More Perfect Nation: Ending Racial Profiling." 41 *Valparaiso University Law Review* 621 (2006).

Kadish, Mark J. "The Drug Courier Profile: In Planes, Trains, and Automobiles; and Now in the Jury Box." 46 *American University Law Review* 747 (1997).

Kennedy, Randall. *Race, Crime, and the Law.* New York: Pantheon, 1997.

Ledwin, Mark G. "The Use of the Drug Courier Profile in Traffic Stops: Valid Police Practice or Fourth Amendment Violation?" 15 *Ohio Northern University Law Review* 593 (1988).

Maclin, Tracey. "Race and the Fourth Amendment," 51 *Vanderbilt Law Review* 333 (1998).

———. "*Terry v. Ohio*'s Fourth Amendment Legacy: Black Men and Police Discretion." 72 *St. John's Law Review* 1271 (1998).

Pew Hispanic Center. "2007 National Survey of Latinos: As Illegal Immigration Issue Heats Up, Hispanics Feel a Chill," December 19, 2007. Available online. URL: http://pewhispanic.org/files/reports/84.pdf.

Ramirez, Deborah, and Stephanie Woldenberg. "Balancing Security and Liberty in a Post-September 11th World: The Search for Common Sense in

Domestic Counterterrorism Policy." 14 *Temple Political & Civil Rights Law Review* 495 (2005).

Rudovsky, David. "The Impact of the War on Drugs on Procedural Fairness and Racial Equality." 1994 *University of Chicago Legal Forum* 237.

Russell-Brown, Katheryn. *The Color of Crime* (2nd ed.). New York: New York University Press, 2009.

Russell, Katheryn K. "'Driving While Black': Corollary Phenomena and Collateral Consequences." 40 *Boston College Law Review* 717 (1999).

Tehranian, John. "The Last Minstrel Show? Racial Profiling, the War on Terrorism, and the Mass Media." 41 *Connecticut Law Review* 781 (2009).

Trende, Sean. "Why Modest Proposals Offer the Best Solution for Combating Racial Profiling." 50 *Duke Law Journal* 331 (2000).

U.S. Department of Justice. "Policing in Arab-American Communities After September 11," July 2008. Available online. URL: http://www.ncjrs.gov/pdffiles1/nij/221706.pdf.

Volpp, Letti. "The Citizen and the Terrorist." 49 *UCLA Law Review* 1575 (2002).

Wilson, Brian A. "The War on Drugs: Evening the Odds through the Use of the Airport Drug Courier Profile." 6 *Boston University Public Interest Law Journal* 203 (1996).

Web Sites

American Civil Liberties Union on Racial Profiling
http://www.aclu.org/racial-justice/racial-profiling
This domestic civil liberties group has many resources about racial profiling, including press releases, lawsuits, detailed reports, and other materials.

Amnesty International on Racial Profiling
http://www.amnestyusa.org/us-human-rights/racial-profiling/page.do?id=1106650
This international human rights group advocates on a variety of issues and also has excellent resources on racial profiling.

Arab American Institute
http://www.aaiusa.org/
This organization is devoted to protecting the rights of Arab Americans. It advocates strongly against the practice of racial profiling.

Daniel Pipes

http://www.danielpipes.org/

> This scholar's Web site has a lot of information about radical Islam, terrorism, and profiling issues.

Federation for American Immigration Reform

http://www.fairus.org

> This organization is devoted to ensuring enforcement of the nation's immigration laws. It seeks to stem the flow of illegal immigration and protect the nation's borders.

Racial Profiling Data Collection Resource Center

http://www.racialprofilinganalysis.neu.edu/

> This Web site created by the Institute on Race and Justice at Northeastern University has incredible amounts of research related to data on racial profiling. It also contains links to various laws on the subject.

PICTURE CREDITS

DAVID L. HUDSON JR. is a First Amendment Scholar at the First Amendment Center at Vanderbilt University. He teaches law classes at Middle Tennessee State University, Nashville School of Law, and Vanderbilt Law School. He is the author or co-author of more than 20 books, including several in the POINT/COUNTERPOINT series.

ALAN MARZILLI, M.A., J.D., lives in Birmingham, Ala., and is a program associate with Advocates for Human Potential, Inc., a research and consulting firm based in Sudbury, Mass., and Albany, N.Y. He primarily works on developing training and educational materials for agencies of the federal government on topics such as housing, mental health policy, employment, and transportation. He has spoken on mental health issues in 30 states, the District of Columbia, and Puerto Rico; his work has included training mental health administrators, nonprofit management and staff, and people with mental illnesses and their families on a wide variety of topics, including effective advocacy, community-based mental health services, and housing. He has written several handbooks and training curricula that are used nationally—as far away as the territory of Guam. He managed statewide and national mental health advocacy programs and worked for several public interest lobbying organizations while studying law at Georgetown University. He has written more than a dozen books, including numerous titles in the POINT/COUNTERPOINT series.